Windsurfing

The Complete Guide

Ian Currer

Published by :

Air Supplies, Dunvegan Lodge, Main St, Barmby Moor, York,
YO42 4EB, UK

© Ian Currer 2004

British Library Cataloguing in Publishing Data

A catalogue record for this book is available from the British Library.

ISBN: 0-9528862-8-6

Text: Ian Currer

Illustrations: David Barber

Page design & layout: Neil Cruickshank

Printed and bound: Perfils, Spain

Front cover photo, courtesy of Gun.

Contents

Acknowledgements

I would like to thank the following people and companies for their invaluable support in producing this book:

Simon Sanderson, Technical Editor (Former UK Speedsailing champion, former technical editor for 'Windsurf' magazine).

Neil Cruickshank for all the layout and organisation.

Dave Barber

Peter Chilvers

Roger Tushingham and all at Tushingham sails.

Starboard

Guy Chilvers and Bic Sport

Brian Johncey at Gun sails

Jacky Bevan for the proof reading

Neilson holidays, and all the staff at Bitez, Gundogan & Vassiliki.

The guys at Grimwith reservoir & Fraisthorpe beach

To all the sailors at the venues above for me poking cameras at them.

Sportif & Club Mistral .

The RYA windsurfing team for the help, information and pictures.

James (for getting me started back in '95).

Jim Glass

Gus of f8 photography and Dave Eberlin for the pics.

Jackie for her patience, support and encouragement.

And all those who supported the book.

Ian Currer July 2004.

Simon Sanderson

Foreword

Windsurfing has certainly changed!

I've been involved with the sport since it's inception, as a participant and competitor, but also as a sailmaker involved full time, with the development of windsurfing equipment.

In the early days the popular image of windsurfing was of people struggling to pull the sail from the water, taking constant duckings and providing much merriment for their 'friends' on the beach. This contrasted with the image of those who could, flying through the air and performing almost superhuman acrobatic manoeuvres. For some it was difficult to make the connection, but many thousands persevered and discovered a new world of freedom on the ocean and a sport that has yet to be equalled by any of the action sports that have come along in recent years.

What's changed? Well thirty years of constant development has certainly changed the equipment, in fact its changed out of all recognition and this has had a major impact on the sport. The boards (including the fastest race boards) are now short and wide, which makes them stable and easy to stand on. The rigs are light and stable, so that, not only are they easy to pull from the water, they're also easy to hold onto when they're up. It's now very easy to learn how to windsurf, with people of average ability quickly reaching a standard that in the old days, took the committed enthusiast many years to achieve.

What remains the same is the sensation of holding the wind in your hands as you skim across the ocean surface, the silver surfer, free as a bird, with only your imagination as the limit of your achievement. Windsurfing is a sport without boundaries, there is always another level, another manoeuvre to be mastered, it's a sport that will never fail to challenge and deliver.

This is what makes Ian's new book so welcome. With the new 'fast track' teaching techniques and modern equipment, many of the older textbooks are now looking decidedly out of date. Windsurfing, at a level that will impress your friends, is now within the reach of most people and what's more it can be achieved in a matter of days and weeks. Ian takes you through the sport in a clear, concise and well ordered manner, which makes this book a great place to start for the 'silver surfer' that lives within us all.

Roger Tushingham July 2004.

Roger Tushingham is a well known and respected figure in the Windsurfing world, his company; Tushingham sails, is recognised worldwide as a leading manufacturer and innovator in windsurfing sail design.

Introduction

There are hundreds of activities, sports and hobbies to choose from! Some sports, like running, cycling or swimming, are predominantly physical; the goal is to get further, faster. Some, like gliding or sub-aqua, appeal primarily on an aesthetic rather than a physical level. Most people are social and competitive to some degree, so it is no surprise that competitive or team games like football, tennis and golf attract millions of players worldwide.

A few sports are strictly for the adrenaline junkies - base jumping, extreme climbing, or snowboarding down mountainsides that even a goat would not go near!

Windsurfing is a sport that offers a unique blend of rewards (and frustration!) on a great many levels.

It is physical, it needs reasonable coordination, and, in some circumstances, it can require considerable strength and endurance - a hard session in waves is a full body workout!

You will inevitably do some swimming, and will get ducked under more than a few times.

Floating around on a light wind day is OK on holiday for a while. But if this is the sport for you, it is only a matter of time before you will find yourself blasting along at high speed, then going for a move which you know full well you may not succeed in pulling off; this does require a fair amount of physical courage.

It is mentally demanding too - a good sailor needs to be able to think ahead, to master some fairly 'technical' moves and understand a good deal about the wind and weather.

Learning to windsurf sets personal challenges that require determination to master. And it offers great satisfaction when you do manage it.

It is also aesthetically pleasing, as the pictures in this book show. Skimming almost silently over the ocean, powered only by the wind on your minimalist craft, is an experience that is appealing on a number of different levels.

Windsurfing can be done all over the world, and there are thousands of great people with whom you can share the experience. It suits a wide variety of ages and abilities, all of whom can gain great pleasure and satisfaction from mastering the skills of windsurfing.

Learning is most effectively done when you have feedback and advice from a competent instructor. But there is a huge amount of useful information that can make the learning process much easier and help your progress, and the beach is not always the best place to absorb this background material.

Many magazines and books are full of a bewildering array of equipment and advice on advanced moves. But the most useful tool to the new windsurfer is an up-to-date guide to dealing with common problems and reflecting the learning experiences of the new sailor.

This book is intended to offer you that handy reference, to address the common problems that are typically encountered, and to help you get going as quickly and effectively as possible.

Getting Started

Learning to master the basics of windsurfing is not very difficult if you have expert help and the right gear.

Both these things are readily available by taking lessons with an instructor at a recognised training centre.

Quite a few people have managed to learn with a bit of advice from their mates. This inevitably takes much longer, and using old kit discarded by experienced sailors or of older design can be a major drawback.

The worst possible method is to start by buying an old windsurfer of unknown vintage from the small ads in your local paper and trying to teach yourself. This method is almost guaranteed to be doomed to failure!

It is a sad fact that as far as the general press is concerned 'suitable for beginners' is a description often applied to windsurfing gear, when 'totally obsolete and hard to use' would be more accurate!

Progress is easy with experienced instructors.

This chapter lays out the basic steps of a typical training programme, and highlights the skills and techniques that are vital to make good progress. It is assumed that reasonably modern kit is available. If not, then you may be better off either purchasing your own or finding a centre that is better equipped.

There are a number of variables to consider before you even begin.

Your teachers or instructors.

Are they capable and qualified? In the UK, and at some centres abroad, the Royal Yacht Association (RYA) issues instructor ratings to suitably qualified people and recognises centres that have shown they have the right personnel, equipment resources, and suitable venue. Between 2004 and 2007, the RYA scheme is changing, and those operating the newer scheme will be designated

RYA 'FASTFWD' instructors and centres. Other countries may have similar national associations, and there are companies such as Club Mistral that have their own instructor training system.

The kit available.

Is it reasonably current? You should be looking at boards that are 170 litres or more in volume and are of the newer 'wide' shape. The ideal is to have a width of at least 75cm., and they will be fitted with a central dagger board or fin. The sails will be constructed mostly of monofilm or laminates and will be fully battened. Race sails with cams are harder to learn with, and should be avoided at this stage. There should be a good range of sail sizes to cater for different pupils and wind conditions. "Soft" dacron sails are fine for a the first day or so but you should be using modern battened sails as soon as you can.

A good selection of equipment (Club Vass) *(Photo: D. Ebberlin)*

The venue and water state.

Bays sheltered from the prevailing wind or beaches with strong waves are bad news. Ideally, your sailing area should be reasonably flat water, and have a good clean wind flow across it.

Lakes or bays open to sea breezes are often a good choice. Salt water is much more buoyant than fresh water, which is a good thing, but on the other hand salt water is more likely to have waves. In all but the shallowest water, buoyancy aids and rescue boats should always be available.

See Chapter 6 for a guide to selecting the right spot.

You need enough space; learning in a bay full of swimmers or boats is not a good idea, and potentially dangerous.

A lockout and rescue boat on hand is a huge advantage. *(Photo: Neilson Holidays)*

Once you are moving along well, you need enough time to relax. You do not want to have to turn immediately to avoid a shoreline or moored boat!

Shallow water is ideal and tends to be warmer, and makes getting back on, or walking back to your start point, practical; but the disadvantages may be that the chance of catching your fin or hitting the bottom if you fall off are increased. If close to the shore, breaking waves are a major disadvantage when learning. If learning on an open body of deep water, a rescue boat on hand is a vital prerequisite.

The school may well have lookout tower, manned to keep an eye on wandering students!

The wind and weather

It is impossible to windsurf in totally calm conditions, but even a fairly light breeze can be used when you are just starting out. Winds that are gusty or very strong simply make progress unrealistically difficult, and often mean rough water as well. Very strong winds are favoured by the experts, but it is wisest to increase your upper limit gradually as your skills improve.

Traditionally, instructors have favoured gentle breezes to start with, allowing time to sort out mistakes and preventing pupils sailing off into the distance. However, if you are reasonably confident, have a good range of sails and modern boards, and do not mind the odd 'high speed dismount'. It has become apparent that you can progress well even if there is a good smooth wind of anything up to around 15 knots 17mph) or so.

In reasonable wind speeds the sail func-

tions efficiently and the board is travelling fast enough to be stable, though the downside is that your arms will soon tire, and sessions should be kept fairly short.

Yourself

The next chapter covers health and safety, and it is worth applying the same critical analysis to yourself as you would to your equipment or to the weather. Most accidents are ultimately caused by human factors, and if you are under-confident or over-confident, cold, tired, ill or hung-over, you are not going to make much progress. If you are physically and mentally prepared to learn, you will make far better progress and get much more from your lessons.

Assuming that everything is in order, your instructor will normally begin by giving an introductory talk on the sport and what you will be aiming to achieve on your initial lessons. This will normally include:

- Introduction to the training centre and him or herself.

- Asking about any related experience that any pupil may have. (Sailing, surfing or snowboarding all require skills that are transferable to some extent). Checking that everyone is in good health and is a confident swimmer.

- Allocation of buoyancy aids, and wetsuits if required

- Introduction to the venue, the boundaries of your training area, any hazards, and how to signal for help.

- An introduction to the kit. Sometimes this will include rigging a sail, but very often the rigs are kept racked up pre-rigged and ready to use.

First lessons

The next step is to be introduced to the basics. This may be done on a land based simulator, or you may get straight into the water.

Your instructor or teacher will usually begin with an introduction to how the kit works. He or she may well demonstrate the basic skills. Climbing onto a board, pulling the sail out of the water (uphauling), turning the board into position by pushing it around with your feet, setting a course by positioning the sail relative to the board, and using power of the wind by trimming the sail correctly. Then the secure position, the importance of keeping your back to the wind and the correct stance, looking ahead, and then sailing a short distance.

Then it is time to try it yourself. It is surprising how easy most people find it to start windsurfing. Of course, you will get it wrong, and you will definitely fall off, but very soon you will master the basics. The key is plenty of practice!

Eventually, when you can sail a course, the next move is to execute a turn - usually a tack (upwind turn) - to allow you sail back the way you came.

You also need to try turning by gybing (downwind turn).

Putting it all together. *(Photo: John Carter, courtesy of Starboard)*

By this stage, you will have fallen off a few times and have had plenty of practice at up-hauling the rig from the water. Once you are able to sail back to your start point with some confidence, you will be ready to start learning some techniques for dealing with more wind.

The key skills are steering primarily by foot pressure, faster tacking and flare gybing.

It is not uncommon for pupils (in any discipline) to find one technique that works and stick with it. However, it is important that you keep trying to expand your range of skills, and practice the stuff you feel weakest at.

As your confidence grows, you will feel able to sail in stronger winds. This is

hard work on the arms and demands a good stance. So the next stage is learning to use a harness. This can be rather traumatic to start with, as a problem that may have resulted in you simply dropping the rig now involves you being pulled forwards into the water by your harness. But once comfortable with hooking in and out, there are huge benefits to reducing the pressure on you arms and helping you get into the correct position to start planing.

Planing is achieved by simply getting the board travelling fast enough to start skimming over the surface of the water rather than pushing through it. Once the board is on the plane it 'comes alive', and is far more sensitive to your foot pressure. Because the craft is now travelling faster through the air and the water and is more sensitive to any input, it is quite common to find you have a few control problems at this stage (a tendency to keep heading upwind is a common example).

Once you have started planing you will spend much of your time trying to get back to that state, and will need to work on your stance, putting adequate pressure through the harness and mast foot and balancing your foot pressure.

Whilst it is perfectly possible to plane fast with a 'clean' board, it is more comfortable and secure if you can locate and use the footstraps, and this is the next exercise to master. Footstraps will have been nothing but a nuisance until this point, but from now on they are invaluable, particularly if you are encountering any chop.

There is some theory to cover while all this is going on - how the board and sail works and is tuned, and correct selection of kit, including fins and different board types.

Choosing a venue, assessing the wind, water state and weather, and learning the rules governing sailing safely with others.

Practical skills like beach starting and self- rescue will also be included, often when conditions are not ideal for planing.

During all these exercises, your instructor will be constantly assessing your progress and ensuring that the key areas of looking ahead, correct balance and stance, sail trim, and controlling the sail's power are coming together properly.

Once planing comfortably and enjoying blasting back and forth across your sailing area, you will find that your performance is rather let down by the slow and awkward turns at the end of each beat.

And there is still the less than appealing prospect of clambering back onto your board to haul the rig up every time you wipe out. The next two tasks are carve gybing and waterstarting. The carve gybe has a number of variations, and you will still need your tacking and flare gybing skills at times, but essentially this is one of the key skills required to windsurf well.

The water start is also vital, particularly if you wish to progress to low volume boards and high winds, and with practice can be a great energy and time saver in the right conditions.

Pretty soon you'll be blasting with the pros

Once you have mastered these key skills you should be able to sail safely in a variety of conditions, use a range of equipment, and know how to get the best from it, and to enjoy the speed and exhilaration of harnessing the wind.

Of course, there is far more progress to be made; you may choose to compete, either in slalom or olympic types races. There are the challenges of wave sailing, or the skills of freestyle to try and master. You may be interested in instructing for a living. (But do not bank on getting rich from it!) Or you may simply enjoy the social side of the sport at your local club, or wish to do a bit of blasting around on holiday.

Windsurfing is a sport that offers you a huge variety of options.

This is a brief overview of the approximate order of progress; some national governing bodies (such as the RYA) lay out a detailed training programme with specified exercises and skills for each level. Or a syllabus may be specified by the school itself.

The basic pattern and core skills remains very similar, with variations depending upon the prevailing weather conditions in the region.

The following chapters deal with each of these areas in turn, and the RYA "Fast FWD" scheme is discussed in more detail in Chapter 24.

A Brief History

Along with the horse and cart, sail power has been the pivotal means of long-distance transport for most of human history. In all that time, it is inconceivable that no-one has used a hand-held mast and small sail to help power their raft or canoe. But until people had enough leisure time to go out for a sail just for the fun of it probably seemed a pretty uncomfortable and impractical idea, and a hand-held sail, whilst OK for drifting downwind, was easily improved by using a fixed mast and a rudder.

The first recorded instances of a sail-powered surfboard were in the 1940's in Hawaii. It may have seemed a good way to add power to progress out through the waves, but the idea never caught on.

The story of modern windsurfing really began in 1958, when Peter Chilvers, then a 12- year-old boy living on Hayling island on the south coast of England, decided to build a new sailing craft for himself. Peter had already made a canoe and sailed small dinghies, and using materi-

Early windsurfers. *(Photo: Dave Ebberlin)*

als he could find and borrow, he made a small craft of very shallow draught with a flat deck.

There was no real space to sit down, but this was no problem to Peter, who decided to sail standing up, and to work the rudder with one foot tied to a long tiller arm.

This was awkward, and was soon abandoned, as the young inventor soon found he could steer by simply tilting the mast and sail backward and forward. The tiller arm was screwed down, leaving the small rudder as a fixed fin.

The mast was made of the wooden shaft of a hooked pole, meant to be used for opening and closing blinds or shop awnings. This was attached to the deck with two linked eye-screws, forming an effective universal joint.

The sail - a triangular section of a tarpaulin, complete with a conveniently-situated clew grommet - was supported by a pair of flat wooden battens, one on each side, that were lashed to the mast - a clamping system that was still in use on production boards 25 years later!

These battens bent in use on both sides as they were loaded by Peter pulling on them, forming a pair of symmetrically curved booms - the arrangement that is familiar to all windsurfers today.

The net result was that all the main elements of a modern windsurfer were incorporated in this simple design.

Peter Chilvers did not know anything about centres of effort or lateral resistance, but he did sail his craft (christened a 'sailboard' by his mother) very successfully for the next two or three years. This included many voyages to watch the Vampyre jets taking off and landing at

Peter Chilvers, aged 12 *(Photo: P Chilvers)*

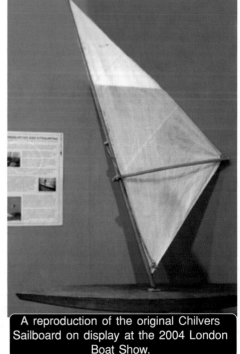

A reproduction of the original Chilvers Sailboard on display at the 2004 London Boat Show.

A couple of old windsurfers propping up a bar

The fathers of windsurfing! Peter Chilvers and Jim Drake in 2004

the Royal Air Force base on neighbouring Thorney Island - a spot from which he was regularly ejected by the base security patrols.

Peter was not just a kid who got lucky, though; he later won a British schoolboys' competition with a catamaran design, and his prize was not only a year's supply of ice- cream, but to be guest of honour on a visit to Thorney Island RAF base!

He later become a successful engineer, and is still a keen windsurfer, instructor and sailor today.

Although Peter Chilvers is unquestionably the first to windsurf in the modern sense, the credit for bringing the sport

to the public is shared by Jim Drake and Hoyle Schweitzer.

By the mid 1960's, surfing was in full swing, particularly in California, and (at least in retrospect) it was almost inevitable that someone would once again try adding a sail to a surfboard. The 'someone' in question was Jim Drake, who came up with the design, and his partner Hoyle Schweitzer. These two put a good deal of work into solving the technical problems, and went as far as going into limited production and lodging a patent for their design. The first modern windsurfer was born. It was not long before the new sport was growing quickly, and the patent, now owned by Schweitzer alone (who had bought out Drake), was registered in several countries. A number of companies began production, and by the late 70's windsurfers were a common sight on beaches all over Europe, as well as the United States.

In an interesting twist to the tale, there was a question over Schweitzer's patent in Europe, and after some prolonged legal battles, in which Peter Chilvers was eventually acknowledged the original inventor, Hoyle Schweitzer's previously lucrative claim to royalties on each unit sold was overturned.

As the popularity grew, so did the skills of the sailors, and the boards and sails progressed rapidly, driven by the demands of competition and a range of conditions.

The standard design soon diversified into recreational boards, racing boards (which were designed principally for good upwind performance) and smaller more agile boards for use in wave conditions. Footstraps were a major change, contributed by the wave sailors of Hawaii, and as sailing in stronger conditions became the norm, the retractable dagger board was introduced; this gave greater flexibility, allowing good upwind progress when it was deployed and easier planing when it was retracted. Sailing in a much wider range of conditions became more practical.

The changes were coming thick and fast in the 80's: small, manoeuvrable designs with no daggerboard, asymmetric board shapes and (with the advent of waterstarting) very low volume boards that allowed sailing in ever-more-radical conditions.

In 1984, windsurfing made the big time and was granted Olympic status. The Olympic recognition was very welcome, however, the racing courses were based on dinghy racing experience, and had to be held on a certain course on a certain day, no matter what the wind strength!

The Olympic criteria of 'no technical advantage from equipment' meant that the Olympics committee had to select a design that was well-established and available everywhere, and to do so several years before the actual competition! As a result, the already outdated 'windglider' design was the first used, and

Mistral 'One Design' racing outfit

to this day the same restrictions of venue and design mean that the Olympic version is still very different from the mainstream sport, though at the time of writing there are discussions taking place on choosing a new design and possibly altering the Olympic criteria to restrict rounds to times and venues dictated by suitable conditions.

As boards grew more sophisticated and

Photo: Darrell Wong courtesy of Starboard

were built from more exotic materials, the sails, too, were evolving rapidly. The earliest sails were sewn from dacron fabric, as used in dinghy sails, often with a mylar or plastic window to help the sailor see where he was going. The addition of battens to the sail reduced flutter and greatly improved efficiency. Before long, full-length tapered battens were the norm, allowing a well-defined airfoil section and further increasing power. Monofilm and the reinforced versions of it become the material of choice for the body of the sail; having no 'weave', it is equally stable and stretch-resistant in every direction, and has the advantage of being transparent. Gradual replacement of glass-fibre masts with carbon/glass composites and lightweight adjustable booms went hand-in hand with the sail development.

By the early 90's, the sport was well established, with national associations, clubs, instructors, magazines on the news stands, and a vast range of equipment to choose from; but as the sport matured, so the articles became more specialised and the kit more expensive. The gulf between the expert or professional sailors doing forward loops or wave sailing Jaws in Hawaii, and the beginner struggling to stay vertical, grew ever wider. At grassroots level, particularly in the UK, the sport was starting to show signs of stagnating.

Some of the major manufacturers have tried to address this in recent years with new boards and rigs that are incredibly light, inexpensive, and easy to sail, and the latest 'super wide' models have scored a great success.

Progressing from total novice to planing at speed has never been so easy. The years 2001 to 2004 has seen the introduction of real performance boards and sails scaled down for the youth market. The National Association's training programmes are being overhauled to reflect the changes and make the sport more accessible to a wider spectrum of people.

In the 80's the typical package holiday offered sunshine, the beach, and little else. But as the demand for activities has grown, so has the trend for many resorts and companies to offer a range of things to keep their clients on the go, and windsurfing has been a favourite holiday option. The boom in foreign travel has been fuelled still further by the growth of the budget airlines (although checking in at the airport with a windsurfer can still be quite challenging!).

As a result, there has grown up a good number of 'vacation windsurfers', who treat the sport the same way as many skiers or scuba divers; learning their initial skills on holiday, and simply brushing up their skills once or twice a year, when they are somewhere with ideal conditions.

This book is also intended as a handy reference for those in that position, who wish to revise their basic skills and knowledge at irregular intervals.

In most good spots with a tourist population you can now find a windsurf school or shop, and the sport is still growing steadily.

The new watersport of Kitesurfing has emerged in recent years, and many windsurfers are also trying their hand at this innovation (with some kitesurfers migrating the other way as well!). This book contains basic details of this new sport, and there is a further book, 'Kitesurfing - *The Complete Guide'*, available for those with a keen interest.

Photo: Bicsport

Health & Safety

Windsurfers exist for just one reason - because they are fun - essentially they are just big toys!

However, the power of the wind and the hazards of being out on the sea are easy to underestimate when we are out playing. Anyone considering windsurfing must bear in mind a few simple safety considerations.

Health

Are you healthy enough to participate? If you are feeling unwell, or are nursing a previous injury, or have some problem that would prevent you from coping with being pulled off the board or being ducked under the water or being able to clamber back on, it is probably wise to give this a miss.

Spot the board! : You do need to be realistic about your abilities and the conditions you sail in.

Once in the water, you may find yourself facing a long swim, and if you keep sailing for long enough, you will certainly experience being ducked only to find you are under the sail when you try and surface. Bruises and scrapes sustained when you are catapulted off the board are unavoidable as you progress to stronger winds.

Obviously, being a reasonable swimmer and at home in the water is a definite prerequisite for a windsurfer.

Medical conditions, such as heart problems or diabetes, may also be a hazard, as your body will be subjected to a great deal of strain, and your energy demands when hammering through rough water at 20 knots are extremely high! Perhaps the most problematical aspect for many people is the fact that you cannot necessarily stop when you have had enough, as you can with some sports. Even if you are cold, tired and waterlogged, you may still need to be able to summon the effort to sail back to your starting point.

General safety

There are three elements to windsurfing safely: the conditions, the kit being used and the human factors of confidence and decision-making.

Windsurfing can be easy; it can certainly look very easy; but do be realistic when deciding what you are capable of - it is better to be on the beach wishing you were out there than out there wishing you were on the beach! This is a sport that requires a good level of confidence and self-belief, but it must be tempered with a realistic view of your own abilities!

In practical terms, you do need to be able to assess the weather situation, and whether your equipment is appropriate: this means the wind strength, the direction, the gustiness, and the state of the water. As in all watersports, it is important that the windsurfer is aware not only of the wave height and direction, but also the state of the tide and currents if sailing on the sea. Water temperature and wind chill are other factors that will determine the safe limit of your time on the water.

Breaking a boom or mast in a strong offshore wind or ebbing tide at the coast is a lot more serious than the same problem on a lake, or with an onshore breeze. In the first circumstance you would need to be much more cautious about, sailing alone or overpowered.

There are further chapters in this book to help you make this kind of evaluation. The best recommendation, however, is to sail with others and take advice from those with the best local knowledge and experience. Never sail in poor visibility, whether caused by poor weather or by dusk; the risks of disorientation and collision are obviously magnified.

If you do choose to sail alone, ensure that there is always someone on land to keep an eye on you, and someone who knows how long you expect to be out. Dealing with problems such as damaged kit is covered in Chapter 13.

5 Introduction to the Equipment

Local sailor Stelios, gives his gear a good workout on an unusually wavy day at Vassiliki Greece.

The Board

There are a huge variety of boards available, constructed in a range of materials.

The illustration shows the basic features of a modern beginner's board, which is quite short, at under 3m. with a width of around 85-100cm. and featuring a retractable (or removable) central daggerboard, or central fin. This is a good option for a new sailor, as these boards are both stable to learn on, and quick and easy for progression to planing at speed when you are ready. (In fact the latest 'formula' racing boards are now using a very similar shape.)

This 'superwide' shape is a fairly recent innovation, and many people are also being trained successfully on slightly older models, which, though still quite wide, are generally longer than the latest designs. In training centres it is common to use very stable boards for a few days and then progress to intermediate boards in a few days, but if buying your own gear at the outset the short broad boards are an excellent choice.

Before the advent of these short, wide, high volume boards, the length was frequently used as an indication of a board's

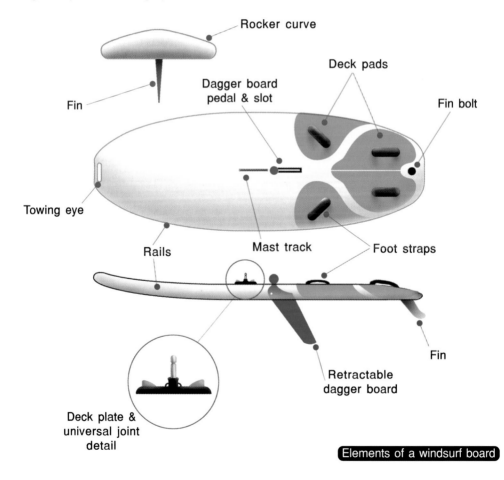

Rocker curve

Deck pads

Dagger board pedal & slot

Fin bolt

Fin

Towing eye

Rails

Mast track

Foot straps

Fin

Retractable dagger board

Deck plate & universal joint detail

Elements of a windsurf board

suitability, and you may still hear sailors referring to 'long' and 'short' boards. 'Long' usually means above 3.2m in length, with a high volume and with a daggerboard, and 'short' means a low volume board with no dagger that is primarily designed for use in planing conditions.

Because it is a better measure of a board's behaviour, it is now becoming more common to refer to a board by its volume (i.e. the amount of water it displaces). One litre of volume will support 1 kilogram (2.2lbs.) of weight, (or a little more in salt water) so this is a handy indicator of the flotation characteristics of the board. A heavier sailor will need a bigger volume for the same buoyancy.

Because the board and the rig themselves weigh perhaps 20kg or more, and you need some buoyancy to spare, the board volume for a beginner should be at least double your body weight in kilograms; i.e. an 80kg. (175lb.) sailor should select a board of 160 litres or more. As you start to sail faster, the board requires less buoyancy to support you, and you can use smaller boards, which are easier to control in choppy water.

On many of the 'next step' boards aimed at the first time buyer who is getting planing, the majority of the volume is located in the thicker and wider section towards the tail. This is so that the sailor can step back and the board will lift onto the plane early; however, if the nose area is very thin or narrow, it is easy for the beginner to sink the nose in waves or when attempting to tack. So before trying one of these it is usually best to get the basics sorted out on a less advanced board. If in doubt, ask an instructor or experienced sailor for advice.

The top surface or deck of the board will have a slightly rough sandpaper-like coating for good grip, or a high-density EVA foam finish. The foam option is much more comfortable when clambering back on to your board (which you will be doing a lot !), but it does tend to be less hard-wearing and not quite as 'grippy' as a hard surface.

Your board may have footstraps screwed to the deck. These are handy for carrying the board to the water, but for the first few days are simply nuisances to the beginner. If you have the option, a good plan is to remove the front pair and leave the back straps just to help manhandle the board.

Boards are constructed in two basic ways. Blow moulded boards have their foam core encased in a moulded plastic skin. This is very tough and resistant to abuse! They are heavier than glass or carbon or wood laminated boards. These boards are commonly found in schools.

The laminated boards are much more fragile, and are more expensive, but they do have a significant weight advantage and this is the most common construction method for more advanced boards.

The board will also feature a mast track to locate the deck plate and mast foot. The track is a slot to enable the mast position to be altered to suit the prevailing conditions, the chosen sail size and the preferences of the sailor.

The daggerboard slot is slightly behind the mast track, and allows the daggerboard position to be adjusted on the water as required. The slot is large enough to conceal the whole daggerboard when it is in the retracted position.

The fin box is a cassette of hard plastic built into the board, so that you can add or remove your fin for transport or for changing type or size. This fin is held in place by one or two bolts recessed into the deck of the board.

The design features and more details about boards are covered in Chapter 10: How the Board Works, and in Chapter 25: Buying your Equipment.

The Fin

Almost all boards will be supplied with a fin, and these will be selected by the manufacturer to suit a specific board in a particular environment. However, the choice of fin is critical in determining the behaviour and performance of the board, so it is worth spending a little time examining the function and different types available. The fin's job is to provide lateral resistance as the board is driven through the water by the sail. Trying to sail without one soon convinces you of the importance of this item, as the board will simply try to skid sideways.

Obviously, the fin is far smaller than the sail, and yet once moving through the water at speed it manages to offer an effective opposing force to keep the board on track. Water is over 700 times as dense as air, so trying to push a fin with an area of perhaps 300-400 square centimetres sideways through it generates a huge amount of pressure, when it is moving forward this is translated into lift.

The line of least resistance for the board, which is being squeezed between this lateral pressure from the fin (and possibly daggerboard) and the force of the sail, is to move forwards.

The fin acts in a very similar manner to the sail, in that the water flow generates a high-pressure area on one side and a low-pressure area on the other. When working hard at speed the fin creates lift, and this helps push the tail of the board higher out of the water. At full speed, perhaps one third of the area in contact with the water is accounted for by the fin, so its contribution is critical.

Because fins are under such high pressures but need to be as thin as possible to minimise drag in a forward direction, they are made of very tough materials to reduce flexing and the risk of snapping. At the stage of being concerned with maximising board performance, the fin choice comes under close scrutiny, and the size and shape can be altered to match the sail size and the sailing conditions, with different variations being available for slalom, wave, or freeriding use.

This subject is mentioned again in Chapter 7.

Windsurfer fin

The Sail

The diagram below shows a typical modern wave-orientated sail.

Sails are constructed from panels of different materials, their selection depending on their intended use. The most common material is polyester monofilm or laminates (see below) with Dacron (woven polyester) fabric for areas subject to the most flexing and abrasion, such as the luff-tube - the sleeve that contains the mast.

Stressed areas are often made with a laminated material such as TriX; this is typically two thin layers of monofilm with a substrate of Kevlar, Polyester or Dyneema (spectra) mesh laminated between them. These sandwich materials are much stronger and more durable, but are also heavier and more expensive. Wave sails may be constructed entirely of various weights of laminate materials.

Clear PVC film may be used for the central 'window' panel; this material is softer and slightly stretchier, minimising the risk of damage caused by your head in this area.

The sail shape is quite complex, including curves in three dimensions. It is supported by a number of battens, which are incorpo-rated into pockets at strategic points. The battens are tapered to curve into predetermined airfoil sections when loaded.

Of course, a sail may be loaded from either side, so the sail and battens must 'pop' through and set correctly both ways.

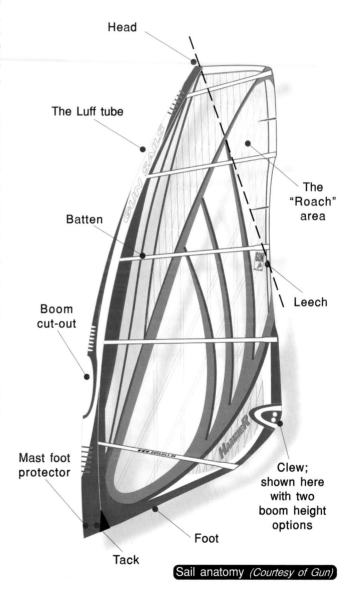

Sail anatomy *(Courtesy of Gun)*

The Mast

Although some cheaper fibreglass masts are available in one piece, most modern rigs use a lightweight carbon and glass fibre composite mast, in two slot-together sections for easy transportation. The stiffness, weight and price of the mast varies, depending on the carbon content, which can be anywhere from 25% to 100%. This data is usually printed somewhere on the lower section of the mast. The IMCS (Indexed Mast Check System) number refers to the stiffness or bending properties of the mast, and each sail is designed to match a certain IMCS range. It is important to the efficiency of the sail that it is correctly set on the right mast, and that includes ensuring that the sail foot is as close to the board as possible.

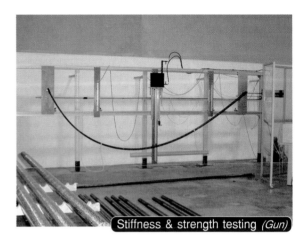

Stiffness & strength testing *(Gun)*

Standard mast (top) and Skinny mast *(Gun)*

Clearly, as there are a wide range of sail sizes, this implies a wide range of mast lengths, which would be rather an expensive proposition. So most masts are too short for the sail when used alone, and are extended to the correct length by using an adjustable mast extension, usually made of aluminium. Combined with the two tapered carbon sections, this allows a reasonable range of sails to be rigged on a single mast (as long as the stiffness is suitable). Smaller sails will feature an adjustable head so that

they can be rigged on an oversized mast.

Each mast features an internally reinforced section designed to withstand the pressure of a boom clamp. Whilst the material used is very strong in flex and longitudinal compression, it is comparatively weak if crushed, so it is important that when the sail is rigged the boom clamp is set within the reinforced section. In practice, this means that each mast will suit a limited range of sails, but if you have a wide selection of sails (a quiver), you may need two or three masts. Real enthusiasts or competitive racers may even have more than one mast for each sail to maximise performance in a range of conditions. Reduced diameter (skinny) masts are also available; these masts have an increased wall thickness to give maximum strength, and combine performance with ultimate flexibility, and are made from stronger stiffer "IM" or "HM" fibre. (Intermediate or high modulus carbon)

The Boom

Made of aluminium or possibly carbon fibre, the boom must also be as light and as strong as possible. The two curved arms of the boom are telescopic to allow extension, so that a range of sail sizes can be used. The boom length is printed on the sails in the same way as the mast data, so that you can set your boom to size before rigging. The booms are connected with a tough plastic fitting at the back (clew) end, and will feature a cord with a pulley or tensioning device and a jam cleat of some type, so that you can adjust and set the outhaul tension on the sail.

At the other end, the booms are connected to a clamp; the designs vary a little, but they all have an adjustable over-centre lever mechanism to ensure that the boom is securely clamped to the mast. A good, secure grip is vital, as the whole weight of the sailor may at times be trying to drag the boom down the mast.

The curved arms of the boom are usually covered in a rubber-like substance to ensure a good grip, and if the sail is used by more experienced sailors there will be harness lines connected on each side to allow them to 'hook in' when necessary.

Telescopic boom

The Mast Foot

This is the piece that slots into the bottom of the mast, to which the tack of the sail is connected. The mast foot incorporates a number of pulleys and a 'downhaul' cord that allows the sailor to thread the sail foot to the mast foot in such as way as to allow a lot of pressure to be exerted.

This bends the mast, and, together with the outhaul on the boom, helps tension the sail to its correct shape.

The bottom of the mast foot incorporates a socket with a quick-release mechanism;

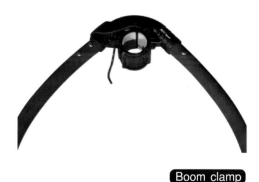

Boom clamp

(From left to right) Pulley, mast extension and pulley hook and mast foot assembly.

this socket accepts the pin from the universal joint of the deckplate and is the method of connecting and disconnecting the sail from the board.

The Deckplate and Universal Joint

The universal joint is based around a tendon of flexible material that allows the sail to be pivoted or moved in any direc-

tion; the top part consists of a grooved stainless steel pin that slots and locks into the mast foot socket.

The lower part houses a bolt with a flat nut that slots into the mast track of the board and can be tightened once in position.

More details of how the equipment is rigged is given in Chapter 7: Setting up your Kit

Deck plate *(left)* and deck plate/universal joint assembly

Other Equipment

Clothing

Rash vests

If you are sailing in the tropics, a nice pair of board shorts or a bikini might be just the thing. However, if it is very warm and you are out for a while, you will probably need protection from the sun, and a rash vest of some type is advisable. These lightweight tops are made of stretch fabrics that cling closely to the skin and do not hold water.

A rash vest will protect you from UV and keep the wind chill to a minimum. They also double as 'underwear' to a wetsuit, adding a little extra insulation in cooler climates. Rash vests are built with the seams on the outside to give the smoothest fit to the skin, and will often feature a high neck line to help prevent chafing from the wetsuit collar as your head moves.

Wetsuits

If you are not quite so lucky in your sailing venue, you will need a wetsuit of some type.

Shorties, made of 1or 2mm. neoprene, are ideal for summer in Mediterranean-type climates.

Convertible wetsuit and rash vest *(Photo: Gun)*

If you are sailing in summer in northern Europe, or somewhere where the water is a bit chilly for swimming for long, then a 3mm. suit with 2mm. arms and legs is likely to be the best choice. Many of these are convertibles, featuring detachable arms, which gives you some scope to regulate your warmth.

Cold water and fresh winds demand a thicker suit. And a 'steamer' with a 5mm. body and 3mm. arms gives a good level of warmth in most spring and autumn conditions. This type of suit is about the limit for allowing freedom of movement, though a few intrepid windsurfers will even go as far as sailing in a dry suit in the winter. If it is really cold, you should consider investing in a neoprene hood or a helmet, as much of the heat lost through wind chill is from your head.

More details on wetsuits are given in Chapter 25: Buying your Equipment.

Footwear

In warm water many experienced sailors prefer to sail in bare feet, as it does give better feedback from the board and makes footstraps work a little easier. But bare feet are more vulnerable to injury from rocks or urchins, or even from your own fin in some situations. They also slide about more easily when you are not

yet using the straps. Note: sun cream on the board or feet is a recipe for disaster in windsurfing!

Most sailors under training use neoprene shoes of some type. These tend to either be the 'surf shoe' variety, that have a number of holes to allow water to flow out; these are primarily for protection when on the beach, and for grip; or the 'bootee' variety, that are essentially waterproof, offering excellent protection, and keeping your feet warm when worn tucked under a full wetsuit.

Ordinary footwear, like sandals or training shoes, is not very suitable, as the feet slide around in them, or they fill with water.

Gloves

In colder weather, gloves are very useful, both keeping you warm and possibly helping with your grip on the boom. Even in warm water, if you are sailing every day, you will soon find that repeated

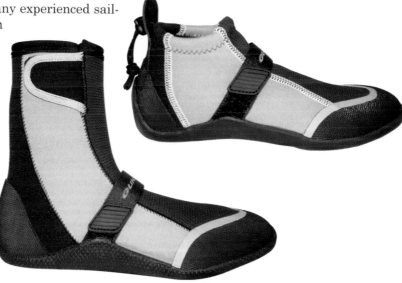

Wetsuit boot and slipper *(Photos: Gun)*

immersion in salt water will soften your skin. Hands that are more used to using a keyboard or doing indoor tasks will soon begin to show signs of wear and tear when you are hauling on ropes and hanging onto the boom.

It is not unknown for sailors, after a couple of weeks of windsurfing every day on holiday, to be driven to visit the local markets to buy rubber washing-up gloves to protect their hands.

There are several types of 'watersport-friendly' gloves, ranging from very thin membranes of fabric or leather, designed primarily for protection against blistering, to neoprene models that are designed for warmth. Gloves should be fingerless and fit snugly.

If sailing in cold water, good gloves are essential, because the elevated arm position (forcing the heart to pump blood uphill) and gripping the boom can constrict the blood flow and cause hands to cool very quickly. Cold fingers are often a key limiting factor in determining your time on the water on cold days. Good wetsuit stores will have a choice of pre-shaped 'steamer' gloves to minimise this problem.

Buoyancy aids

The choice to use a buoyancy aid is usually left to the individual. You will be falling off, and they do reduce your risk of going right under the surface. They also help protect your chest from impacts and scrapes when climbing back on. But perhaps the main use is simply to aid confidence in the water, especially if it's wavy, or if you have to wait to get rescued. Because you are higher in the water, you are also more visible to others.

Using a buoyancy aid is recommended when you are learning to water start, as it does help a great deal whilst you are perfecting your technique.

A wetsuit does give some additional buoyancy anyway; so does a harness, particularly if you are sailing in sea water, and of course the board itself is a big float; for these reasons, many instructors will allow confident sailors to learn without a buoyancy aid if they wish, though they should always be available if requested. Children should always use one, and it is important that they are the correct size and do not 'ride up' over the head in the water.

Note : A waist harness cannot be used with some buoyancy aids, so if you are not very confident in the water and would prefer to use one, choose a seat harness when you reach that stage.

Helmets

These are becoming a more common sight; initially used by wave sailors, who were experiencing cracks on the head by the board or mast when wiping out, they are also useful for keeping your head warm. The type with a visor even allows you to see clearly when a wave is breaking over your head! Most sailors have had a bump at some time and being stunned for a few moments can be very bad news if you are face down in water. A helmet is rapidly becoming a regular piece of equipment, and is essential in waves.

There are specific designs for surfing, kitesurfing or windsurfing use. These offer a close fit in the manner of a wetsuit, are light, have ear-holes to ensure hearing and balance are not compromised, and have quick-release chin straps.

Types designed for dry sports are not usually suitable, as the looser fit and foam and fabric linings mean they collect and absorb water.

Sailors in cold climates may use a neoprene hood to keep their heads warm; these are very effective, and in extreme conditions can be teamed with a helmet.

Long hair can be a nuisance when windsurfing; it can be a real problem when learning if it gets in your eyes and you don't have a hand free to move it back. Some kind of tie-back is vital to keep longer hair out of your face when sailing.

Helmets are also good for covering any bald spots!

Harnesses

You do not need a harness during the initial learning period; they simply get in the way and the hook can even damage the board as you climb on. However, the force of the sail in a strong breeze is enough to propel you and your windsurfer to well over 20mph over the water. Much of this force is transmitted from the sail, through your arms and shoulders, and down your back to your legs and feet, which in turn push the board along. This is hard work, and using a harness cuts out the weaker part of your body (the arms and upper back) and transmits the power directly from your sail through your hips and to the board. For this reason, all sailors who reach the stage of planing regularly will need to use one.

(Left to right) Purpose designed helmet, seat harness, waist harness

Harnesses come in two main varieties: seat and waist. The seated type allow the sailor to lean back to a more radical angle, and the hook is set a little lower. They can be used with a buoyancy aid, and because they have straps around the legs, cannot ride up in use. This type dominated for many years and is still popular with sailors who have been at the game for some time and are used to them.

Waist harnesses have become much more popular in the last few years, driven initially by their use for wave sailing, where the higher hook position and more upright stance was important. For the same reasons, they are also a little easier for most beginners, and as a result, most sailors now learn on, and subsequently stick with, a waist harness. They are quick to put on and take off, as there are no leg straps, and slightly better as flotation aids, as they are worn above the body's centre of gravity.

Learning to use the harness is covered in more detail in Chapter 14.

Equipment Protection

Although they are very strong when used on the water, the search for lower weight has meant that many modern boards are now often quite fragile when subjected to knocks or scrapes. A padded board bag is a good idea to protect your investment, and makes it easier to load boards onto your roof rack. They are especially important when travelling with your kit.

There are a few other protective items are worth mentioning, A mast foot protector, typically a disc of rubber that slips over the deck plate and minimised stubbed toes.

A boom protector, or "boom bra" is a padded sleeve that fits over the clamp, and is primarily for protecting your head and the nose of the board when wiping out!

The trend for lighter board construction and little volume at the nose does mean that some boards have relatively fragile nose areas and if the sailor is catapulted in a good wind, the mast can whack this area pretty hard and cause some dam-

Boom protector and board fitted with nose protectors and 'Jez's knob' mast deflector.

age. There are a couple of items that can minimise this risk.

A foam "bumper" on the nose is offered as an option on some new boards, or you can fit a deflector of some type to the mast track.

The deflectors work by knocking the mast to one side as it comes down, or deforming under the load, avoiding or minimising impact with the nose of your board.

They are fitted into the mast track in the same way as the deckplate itself, and are located just ahead of the mast. This does mean that they could get in the way of your feet when tacking, and could foul the mast when you are moving it around horizontally when manoeuvring the rig to waterstart. On some boards, the loss of the first few centimetres of mast track adjustment can be a problem if you like to set your mast foot well forward.

6 Understanding the Wind & Water

Windsurfing is only possible by harnessing the power of the wind, so in order to do it well, it is important to understand a little about the wind and how it behaves. Will it increase later, or change direction? Will the airflow be smooth or turbulent? Is there a spot that is better for launching?

This is crucially important to us, so the more we understand about the wind's behaviour the better we can predict and make the most of it.

The Wind

Wind is the name we give to a moving air mass. The air mass can be quite small or it can be very large. However, whatever the size, it has mass and is therefore affected by gravity, making it tend naturally to sink towards the surface. It also has inertia, and once it gets moving one way, it tends to carry on until something stops it.

The big picture: when the sun warms the earth's surface, this heat is transferred to the air lying on the surface; the molecules become more active in their movements, bounce off each other more strongly and therefore take up a greater space. This expanding air becomes lighter; the pressure becomes lower; it can hold more water vapour and it will tend to rise. Any cooler, heavier air ly-

ing on water or in shade, for example, will now flow into the low-pressure area, and we feel the flow as wind.

Differential heating between different parts of the earths' surface causes this basic pattern, which may be on a small scale as localised thermals, on a larger scale as a sea breeze developing on a coastline, or on a global scale, with trade winds blowing between permanent weather cells. Just to make this more interesting, half the world is in darkness and therefore cooling down at any one time, and the whole globe is spinning at 650mph. The result is that weather patterns can be quite complex, and that the wind, rather than moving in a straight line, will tend to travel in a curve. For our purposes, we need to know a little about the weather systems that affect our sailing conditions, and a good grasp of the features of a synoptic chart (pressure map) as used on the more detailed TV or fax forecasts is invaluable.

This topic is covered in more detail in Chapter 20. Our more pressing concern however, is: once you are on the beach, is the wind OK?

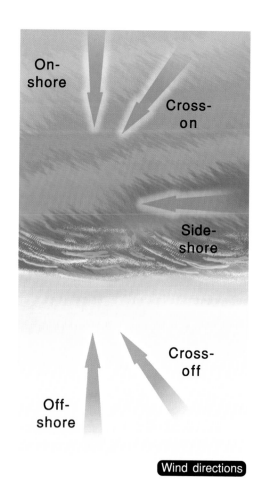

Wind directions

Wind Direction

The first consideration is direction. Until you are pretty competent, have a rescue boat following you, or are sailing in an enclosed area of water like a lake, the wind should be on- shore or side-shore (blowing parallel to the beach) to some degree. For beginners, who are likely to progress downwind on each beat, a perfect side-shore or side-on-shore is ideal.

Once you are confident of returning to your start point then some offshore component becomes acceptable. A directly onshore wind may be a little difficult to

use, as you will keep finding yourself back on the beach. An offshore wind may be dangerous without a rescue boat, as you have the opposite problem - you will keep finding yourself travelling out to sea.

Wind Strength

The second variable is strength; if the wind is very light, you will not move very fast and will not be able to lean back against the pull of the sail. The board will be very unresponsive to inputs. The fin in particular is designed to function best at speed, and, like an aircraft wing, it will only work if it is moving! Because the fin cannot generate much pressure, the board will tend to drift downwind. This is also true to a lesser degree for a daggerboard.

If the wind is strong, power will not be a problem, but maintaining control might be; you can try using a smaller sail if one is available, but high winds also mean choppy water, and if you are consistently overpowered it can be hard to learn anything useful.

The optimum wind range for beginners is 5-15 knots[+] With more experience, this range will increase. The size of sail and design of board also have a bearing on the useable range of conditions - for example a shorter board with no dagger will not work as well in light winds as a longer board.

Turbulence

The third variable is the consistency of the wind; those breezes flowing over large bodies of water like the sea are often quite smooth, but when they have been flowing over land, particularly high terrain like mountains or cliffs, the flow can be turbulent.

Wind behaves almost like a liquid in its flow patterns, pouring down over cliffs and 'rotoring' behind obstacles. Inland bodies of water like lakes or estuaries, especially those surrounded by hills, trees or buildings, can suffer from 'bad' air, making windsurfing more difficult. Even at sea, if you are sailing close to a headland or an island, or even a harbour wall or a vessel that is upwind of you, you can expect the wind to curl around

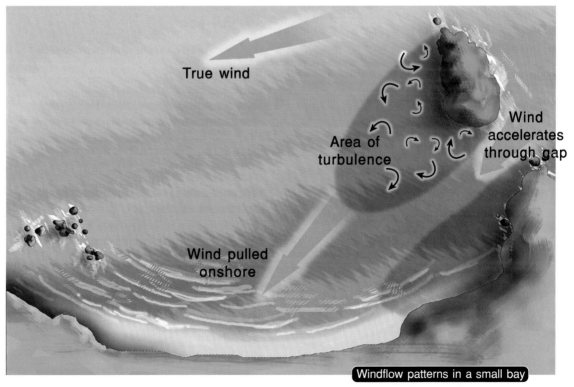

True wind

Area of turbulence

Wind accelerates through gap

Wind pulled onshore

Windflow patterns in a small bay

[+]*A knot is the standard measurement of speed on the water and is used to give windspeeds in all marine weather forecasting. A knot is one nautical mile per hour, and a nautical mile is about 1.15 miles or 1.85 kilometres.*

Airflow over the landscape

it and become unstable, with dead patches and gusts as you get closer to the obstacle.

It could be a bit embarrassing to be blasting past a ferry-load of admiring tourists when you are suddenly de-powered and fall off! Try and visualise the airflow towards you, so that you are ready to avoid or make the most of any changes.

Unstable air with convection currents (thermals) can also cause gusty winds, and a thermic flow is often characterised by sudden changes in direction, too. Apart from the character of the wind, convection is often marked by cumulus clouds in the sky, circling birds, and by darker patches of water where the thermal gusts ruffle the surface.

Approaching weather fronts and squalls can also change the strength and character of the wind in just a few minutes. As a rule of thumb, if the wind speed is varying by 100% or more in less than one minute, it is going to feel very rough, and it may prove very hard to keep good control.

Wind assessment is important when you are choosing your start point; a cross-shore wind may well mean that parts of the beach are in turbulent air or wind-shadow from a nearby hillside or headland.

Tides & Rips

Tides

Another extremely useful piece of information you will need if sailing on the coast is the state of the tide.

Tide tables can usually be purchased locally from a chandler's or harbour master's office, on the internet, or checked by phone with your local windsurf shop - this information is also given on some automatic weather station readouts.

The time of the highest tide moves back by roughly three-quarters of an hour each day, and a complete cycle from high tide to high tide takes around six hours.

This means that if you sail a certain beach at low tide at, say, 12am one Sunday, and go back at the same time the following Saturday, you can expect to find that the tide will be close to its highest.

Tides are caused by the gravitational effect of the moon and sun distorting the surface of the sea. Large bodies of water, like the Atlantic or Pacific Oceans, have moderate tidal ranges, but smaller bodies, such as the Mediterranean or the Red Sea, have only a small range. The biggest ranges are found when a smaller sea is connected to a larger ocean, (the North sea for example) in these cases the tidal flow resonates with the larger body of water but in a confined area, and the tidal range can be very large.

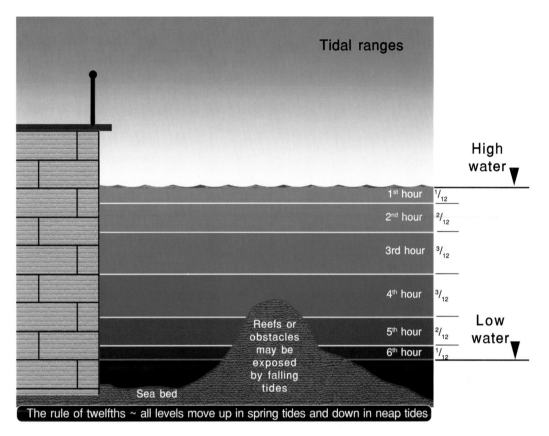

Tidal ranges

High
water ▼

1st hour	$^1/_{12}$
2nd hour	$^2/_{12}$
3rd hour	$^3/_{12}$
4th hour	$^3/_{12}$
5th hour	$^2/_{12}$
6th hour	$^1/_{12}$

Low
water ▼

Reefs or obstacles may be exposed by falling tides

Sea bed

The rule of twelfths ~ all levels move up in spring tides and down in neap tides

The tides are caused by sun and the variations in tidal height are affected by the moon phase. The highest tides are caused when the moon, earth and sun are all lined up on one axis.

These are known as spring tides (even though they do not occur only in spring!)

When the moon is at right angles to the earth-sun axis, the tidal ranges are at their lowest, and these are known as neap tides.

A windsurfer normally moves relatively fast and has only a small wetted area affected by the motion of the water. But the tide is still an important consideration to all sailors, for a number of reasons. A falling tide means that hazards like submerged rocks can change from being unimportant to dangerous in the space of half an hour; beaches can disappear completely; and the condition of the water and waves at the shoreline can also change significantly.

If the wind is light and you are only moving slowly, an ebbing tide can be dangerous, as it can move you offshore at a significant speed.

Tides are not just the rising and falling of the water level - they are also responsible for tidal streams, which can travel at speeds of several knots along the coastline.

On many beaches, especially those with a steep or varying angle of slope, the state of the tide can have a huge bearing on the state of the waves and water. Tumbling waves or rips on the steeper shore at high tide may affect a beach that is easy to start from at low tide.

Rips

A rip is a defined current that usually follows a channel on the sea-bed and acts like a river, draining the water from the waves and tides back out to sea, sometimes at surprising speed. Rips are hard to identify, and you may sail right over them many times without problems, only discovering the drift out to sea when you have fallen off your board or the wind has dropped. Because a rip is effectively a defined current, the best way to escape from one is not to try and swim or sail directly against it, but to move sideways until you are free of its influence before trying to come ashore. In these situations it is important to stay with your kit, as waves and rips can soon separate you from the board. Which is bad news for you and for your gear.

On beaches protected by a reef, the sheltered lagoon often gives excellent flat water blasting conditions, but the water entering the bay as the waves break over the reef has to escape somewhere. There is often a narrow and quite powerful rip flowing outward through a gap or channel in the reef. Always treat such areas with great caution.

If sailing a new beach it is always worth getting local advice on the conditions.

If you do find yourself coming in to land in an area of turbulent water, broken waves or strong rips and backwashes from waves, take some time to plan your approach, and time your landing between sets of waves; or if necessary sail away to a friendlier spot to come in.

Always get yourself and your kit out of the water quickly.

In certain areas, such as estuaries, the tide state can create strong onshore, long-shore or offshore drifts. This can make the difference between safe enjoyable sailing or struggling to tack upwind a long way. The canny sailor can sometimes use these currents to his advantage in making progress upwind.

The difference between a safe and enjoyable windsurfing session and a nightmare of struggling for control can easily be down to your assessment of the conditions, so it is worth your while to check the forecasts, be careful, and quit if it feels too much for you.

Further information on wave formation and sailing in waves is covered in Chapter 22.

Setting Up Your Kit

The Board

Before you lift a board from the rack or untie it from your car, try and locate a good spot for rigging your kit. This will often be the beach, but grass is much better if you can find a patch. If the ground is rough or abrasive (like a car park!) and you are fitting fins or footstraps, it is a good idea to place the board on top of a board bag.

You may only have access to one board to start with, especially if you are using your own kit, so your choices are a bit limited; but a school may have a good range, so (just for the purposes of this discussion) let's assume you have an unlimited choice!

If you are complete novice, you should be using either a large 'widestyle' beginners board, fitted with a retractable daggerboard (2 below), or a new 'superwide' board, with an elliptical shape and either a daggerboard or a fixed central fin (1 below).

Initially the board should be used with the daggerboard permanently down (fully

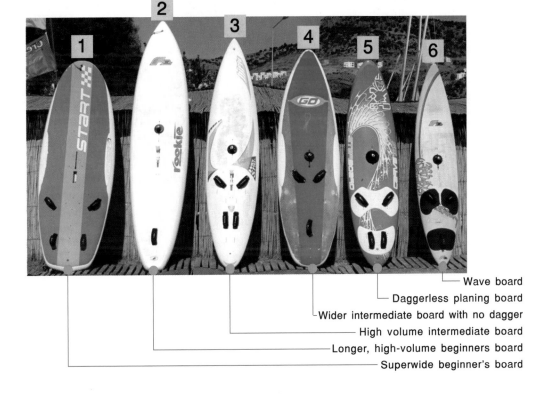

Wave board
Daggerless planing board
Wider intermediate board with no dagger
High volume intermediate board
Longer, high-volume beginners board
Superwide beginner's board

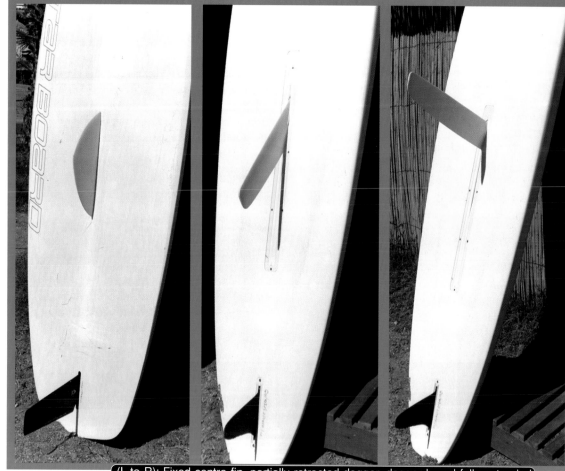

(L to R): Fixed centre fin, partially retracted dagger, dagger board fully extended

extended), or, if it has a central fin, this should be fixed for the first stages of your training. This makes the board more stable and easier to sail upwind (so that you will drift less). The only downside to daggers and central fins is that they create drag and reduce performance a bit, but this is a minor consideration at this stage.

If you are planing (or about ready to plane) then you may choose a slightly smaller and lighter board in preference to a complete beginner's setup or the older, longer boards (3 or 4 above). There are a huge number of models, so it is impractical to refer to specific names. However, a board with a volume of 160 litres or more, a length of around 3m or so and a width of around 70cm. will probably offer you the best compromise between stability and the ability to uphaul the sail and early planing characteristics.

Some of these may have a daggerboard fitted, but many will not. Note: it is unwise to try and sail in very light winds without a daggerboard or central fin, as it much harder to maintain an upwind heading.

If you are already sailing well enough to confidently hold a course, are moving at a reasonable speed, can tack and gybe and are ready to progress to flare gybes, you can start to experiment with retracting the dagger board for the more downwind portions of your sailing - or using a board without a dagger at all. Early planing boards (like 5 above) are ideal.

If you are getting into the straps and blasting at speed, but it is a bit choppy or wavy, you will soon find that the light wide boards that are so good for getting planing are hard work to keep stuck to the surface. The nose is light and rears up when the wind gets under it as you chop-hop. It is a strain to keep the mast foot loaded when you are hanging so far back, and if you relax, the board may start to weave. In these conditions (provided you are waterstarting confidently) you need to select a lower volume board.

This will be easier to control and will cut through the chop. If you do get airborne it is much easier to fly too... you might start thinking about a low volume board (like 6 above). In serious waves you must have a dedicated wave board and fin. More information on boards and other kit is in Chapter 25: Buying your Equipment.

The Fin

If your board does not have the rear fin fitted, this must be attached. The fin usually slots into a tough, plastic box moulded into the underside of the board at the tail, and is held in place by a bolt (or two) that is tightened by an Allen key or screwdriver. The bolt head will usually be in a recess in the deck and must be sufficiently tight. Note: always keep your Allen key or other tools with your fins!!

The fin is designed to fit tightly, and any sand or grit must be rinsed out of the box, and the fin wiped clean before fitting. Otherwise, you risk damaging the fin and board, or suffering from the fin getting jammed. If you have a choice of fins, you will need to refer to your board manufacturer's recommendations on which is best.

A fin is designed to balance the power of the sail, and

with boards with no dagger, a good rule of thumb is to multiply the sail size in square metres by 5, then add 3 to give a minimum fin length.

e.g: a sail of 5.0m x 5 = 25 + 3 = 28, so you would need a fin of at least 28cm. in length. By using this formula, you soon find that a big sail needs a huge fin! Many sailors compromise with 25-35cm. fin for normal use and a 40-50cm. fin if they are using big sails. There is more information on fins in Chapter 10.

Of course this does not make any allowance for the twist in the sail, the width of the board or changes in water density. But unless you are really interested in the math, or a serious competitor or chasing speed records, the best advice is to stick with what the board manufacturer recommends.

The Deck Plate and Universal Joint

In the case of a school where the boards are racked up near the water, the deck-plates and UJs are often left connected. (See pic) However, they must be removed for transport, so will need to be re-attached if the board has been moved.

The board will feature a recessed slot that the deck plate will slide along. Most systems use a flat nut that remains on the protruding bolt of the deck plate.

The bolt and nut are inserted into the slot and moved to the desired position, then locked by tightening the thread - usually by rotating the plastic body or skirt of the deckplate until the nut is gripped tightly in the slot. Some boards use a different mechanism where the deckplate has to be captured with a pin or spring of some type.

Some older long boards may still feature sliding deck plates that can be adjusted whilst sailing by depressing a foot pedal.

Each manufacturer has their own system, and these are not all compatible, so a deckplate and Universal joint (UJ) from one board will often not fit another. Even more annoyingly, you can have a fully rigged sail and a board with a deckplate and UJ, but because the groove in the UJ pin, or the pin diameter is a couple millimetres different, the system is not compatible. More than one sailor has bought second-hand kit only to find he then has to buy new deckplates or mastfeet to be able to use it with his existing gear. If you have just bought some new bits, try putting it all together before going sailing.

Boards being stored with U.J's fitted

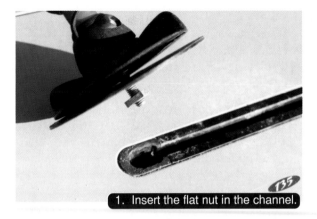

1. Insert the flat nut in the channel.

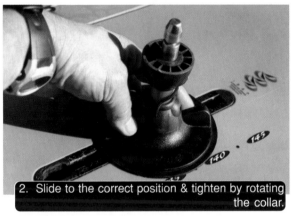

2. Slide to the correct position & tighten by rotating the collar.

'locked' in the straps, the mast foot can be moved back slightly towards the rear of the board. This is, however, not an absolute rule; it is true that some boards have different characteristics and if you use a smaller sail this can be the other way around. The good news is that many sails will come with advice on optimum mast track position.

The Sail

If there are windsurfers already out when you arrive at the beach, the first move is to check what size sails those who have already been on the water are using.

'What size are you using?' is a standard international greeting among windsurfers, and it is always worth seeing what the locals are doing, even if it is just to confirm your decision!

Once you (or your instructor) have decided on a sail, it may need to be rigged. In many holiday resorts sails are stored fully rigged, making this step easy, but at some point you will need to rig your own.

The board offers you a track with multiple positions for the mast foot. Where should it be located? For beginners or intermediate sailors the mast foot should be positioned near the centre of the track. The standard measurement on modern boards is about 135cm from the tail. This is often marked on the mast track for easy location.

In lighter winds where the board is just coming onto the plane, the mast foot can be moved forward if required, as it will help the sailor to maintain mast foot pressure and a flat board as his feet move back. In stronger conditions where the sail is raked backwards and the sailor is

Here is the step by step guide:

1

Unroll the sail on the smoothest piece of ground available. (Grass or sand is ideal). You should unroll it so that the bottom (tack) of the sail is pointing roughly into the wind. On some older sails a batten may need inserting, if so fit them before putting the sail onto the mast.

2

Read the mast data (printed on the sail) and select a mast of the correct length and stiffness.

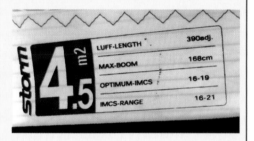

3

Assemble the mast and mast extension to the correct length. There are two ways to make a sail fit a mast neatly, if an extension is needed, then set the head adjustment so that there is no mast protruding at the top. Then use the extension to set the mast length and downhaul the sail until the pulleys are almost touching and only the last couple of centimetres of mast foot is protruding.

If the mast is too long, the excess should be clear of the sail head at the top and the tack of the sail should again be almost flush with the bottom of the mast foot.

This ensures that the sails' centre of effort is kept low, that the sail will be easier to handle and uphaul and the boom clamp will be well positioned on the mast.

4

To rig the sail, slide the mast into the luff tube of the sail. Because the luff is built in a curve, you may have to 'scrunch' then heave the sail few times to get the mast right up to the head. Freeride sails are usually quite easy, but race sails featuring battens with camber inducers (cams) can be a struggle to locate well, and these may need pushing up the mast individually.

Slide the mast in, then 'scrunch and heave' the sail down into position.

If a cam jumps off the mast you may have to go back a few steps to spring it back on..

5

Insert the mast foot and thread the downhaul cord through the pulleys; pull the downhaul enough to get the foot of the sail reasonably close to its final position. This will locate the cut-out in the luff tube on the correct area of the mast to enable you to connect your boom.

Fitting a pulley hook to the tack of the sail

Using a 'grunt tool' to downhaul

6

Check the length of the boom is correct (the measurement will be given on the sail). If not, there will be some scope for adjustment with the telescopic arms. Slip the boom over the foot of the sail and move it into position with the clamp in the luff-tube cut out. Many sailors mark the mast at their favoured boom height to make this easier.

A good way to check boom height is to note where the boom lies in relation to the tail of the board when rigged.

The boom height is dependent on the footstrap position for planing use, so no matter what board you are using the correct height will always be the same distance from the tail of the board.

7

Clamp the boom tightly - it must not slip down, even with all your weight hanging from it! Only a specific section of the mast is sufficiently reinforced to accept the boom clamp. Make sure your boom is located in this area.

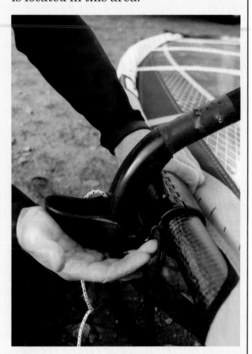

Tensioning the outhaul

Setting the outhaul is normally quite simple, the Sail will have recommended boom measurement as well to work to. Thread the outhaul cord and apply enough pressure to ensure the sail is not touching the booms. If the boom is the correct length, the clew of the sail should be within two centimetres of the boom end. The pressure required for outhauling is minimal compared to the downhaul; it is a common error to pull too hard.

8

Go back to the downhaul and give a final pull to set the sail fully. *(Note: modern sails need a very powerful downhaul.)* At least a 6 to 1 advantage from a pulley system is necessary and a 'grunt' tool, or other rigging device, like a harness bar, will prevent the cord digging painfully into your hands, and is a big help. In sharp contrast to the outhaul, it is quite rare to be able to downhaul too much! The 'tack' or foot of the sail should be very close to the bottom of the mast extension. The correct tension can be checked in a number of ways, the easiest being that many sails now have stickers with advice on where creases should occur.

Using a harness hook to downhaul a sail and *(inset)* a 'grunt tool'

When you have finished, the body of the sail should look clean, with the luff-tube taut against the mast and the lower battens overlapping the mast by less than 50% of its diameter (some will be fully clear). The top battens should not touch the mast. If you grasp the luff tube at a point about 70% of the way up the mast, you should be able to rotate it slightly.

The 'roach' of the sail at the head may look a bit floppy and perhaps even have some soft folds; this is normal. (Some sails may have a small horizontal adjustment at the head to allow you to tension this area separately.)

If there are wrinkles or stress lines on the sail, it indicates that something is not right. The stress-lines tend to point at the problem area, such as an over-tensioned outhaul.

The rigged sail

Tuning the Sail

Wrinkles tend to run at 90 degrees to the problem area, and usually mean that more tension is required.

Wrinkles that cannot be tuned out by outhauling or downhauling may be related to batten tension. Most modern sails are delivered already set up with the battens tensioned properly, but if you do need to tighten them, you should do so in small increments, as it is possible to damage the pockets. There are different systems of tensioning battens and most will require an Allen key or other tool.

Slightly less downhaul and outhaul will give a deeper section to sail when loaded, which is good for generating extra power (especially at lower speeds). A slightly tighter, flatter sail, with a looser roach is better for top speed and control in stronger winds.

Boom Height

This is a matter of personal preference; for your initial training it is better to have the boom a bit on the low side - that is around 10cm. below your shoulder level. This is a comfortable position for many novice sailors. However, as you start to use stronger winds and use a harness, the boom height should be raised to around chin height (top of the shoulders).

To check your boom height you either need to attach your rig and get onto your board, or stand the mast foot on the ground and mentally add the height of the UJ. If you are at a school they may have a UJ bolted to a piece of wood or metal that you can use to help you set your boom height.

As soon as you are using a harness, the position of the hook and the length of the harness lines will become the deciding factor.

Standing a mast foot directly on a sandy or gritty beach is asking for trouble; the particles will get packed in the socket and may cause it to jam or release prematurely.

Adjusting the boom with the sail set is perfectly possible, but it is much easier

Boom height checking. This boom is just touching the tail of the board - just right for a sailor of about 5'10" (1m 78cm). A 6'3" (1m 90cm) sailor will need the boom set about 2" (5cm) higher, a 5'4" (1m 63cm) sailor about 2" (5cm) lower...

Checking boom height on board, this boom is too high, it should be at around shoulder height

Getting it all into the water

You will see expert sailors nonchalantly pick up their boards and rigs together and amble to the water's edge, drop the board in, step on and sail away. In fact this exercise (like so many others!) requires a mixture of the right gear and a practised technique. You are likely to be using a bulkier and heavier board to begin with, and the easiest way to move it is without the sail. Because a board has a relatively large surface that catches the wind, it is best carried with the nose or tail directly into the wind or held horizontally to minimise the area the wind can push against. This may even mean carrying it balanced on your head; if possible, a good solution is to carry two boards between two people.

Before leaving your board, make sure it is out of the reach of the waves and park it tail into wind.

Once your board is parked at the water's edge, you can go back for your sail. Hopefully it is where you left it, but sails have a nasty habit of taking flight by themselves when left unattended, so placing it foot into wind in a sheltered spot and

to do on the beach than bouncing around in waves. Release the boom clamp slowly and knock the boom up or down the mast with your hand or knee. Be careful - if the clamp comes off the mast you may have to release the outhaul to get it back on.

putting something heavy like a rolled up sail (not a sharp rock) on top of it is a wise precaution. If it is very breezy, you may need to use the uphaul rope to tie it to something while you leave it.

Carrying the rig poses similar challenges to carrying your board; keep it flat if possible, and walk with the leading edge of the airfoil (the mast) into the wind. As the rig will generate lift, you can use this to help you carry it! In lighter winds it is often easiest to simply carry it on your head and stabilise it with one hand on the boom and one on the mast.

If you have a light board or are reasonably strong, you might try carrying the board and rig together. Attach the rig, and lay it back along the board and slightly to one side. Stand between them and hold the board by a foot strap and the rig by the boom. With a bit of practice this method can work well (as long as you are not trying to walk downwind.)

he easiest way to carry a rigged sail any distance

55

Polyethylene blow-moulded boards will stand being dragged over sand a short distance, but never drag a composite board, as the surface will be damaged very easily.

Parking a board and rig together. Always arrange the sail so that the mast is pointing downwind. Then (without detaching it), invert the board and lay it at 90 degrees to the sail, pinning the mast foot to the ground.

When you get changed into your wetsuit and harness depends on your sailing venue. If it is a long walk to the sea, then it is obviously better to carry your gear all ready to go. However it may be more comfortable to get rigged in your clothes, then park the kit whilst you change.

Most wetsuits have a small pocket sewn in near the main zipper to allow storage of a car key, or you may prefer to hang your key around your neck on a cord. (Tuck it inside your suit or rash vest, or

Sliding a Blow-moulded board over sand

it could catch on a boom clamp or other obstruction when you come off). Bunches of keys are a problem, so it is well worth taking just your spare if you are travelling alone (or if your companion is likely to wander off while you are sailing!).

Put your harness on if you are using one, ensure the strap ends are all tucked away, the bar is tight, and that it is at the right height for the harness lines.

Once suited up, it is time to get into the water. But just before you do, quickly check:

- If you are using a harness, ensure it is done up tightly with any loose straps tucked away.
- If you are wearing a buoyancy aid as well, check it is correctly done up and make sure it does not obstruct your harness hook.
- If it is the first time you have used that rig that day, check your boom is the right height.
- The wind has not changed.

To connect your rig to the board, lay the rig with the head pointing away from you on the leeward (downwind) side of the board, tip the board onto its side and reach over to access the mast foot, which you can pull onto the UJ protruding from the deck.

You should feel it click into place, but always give it a good tug just to make sure.

Check that the uphaul rope is connected to the mast foot (usually they have a loop that is simply placed over the mast foot or UJ before clipping the rig on).

With the board in deep enough water, you can manually push the daggerboard down before climbing on. Or you can get onto your board and sail it into deeper water before using the instep of your back foot to push the protruding head of the daggerboard forwards, into the fully extended position.

You are now ready to go windsurfing.

Note: it is always worth re-checking that your UJ is firmly connected and in good condition before launching!

Basic Control

There are a number of core elements involved in successfully controlling a windsurfer.

You need to get a feel for it and establish reasonable balance on the board, and to look ahead and orientate yourself with the horizon and the direction of travel; to be able to control the direction of the board, and to manage the power generated by the sail.

Of course, all these elements are linked - looking ahead aids balance, for example, and the power from the sail dictates your foot and body position to keep the board properly trimmed.

A bird does not know how it flies, or a dog how it runs, and it is true that you do not need to be conscious of any of these aims - most of the skills will eventually be learned unconsciously by your brain and muscles as you practice.

However, if you are aware of these goals and understand the processes involved, it can help speed your progress and it will help you identify and correct any problems you encounter.

You will soon be up and away *(Photo: Bicsport)*

Putting it into Practice

When you climb onto the board for the first time, it will feel quite unstable.

It moves under your feet, and it will take some practice to balance comfortably.

When you grasp the outhaul rope and start to pull the sail up, this initially helps your balance since the rig acts as a counterweight that you can move in the same way as a trapeze artist uses a long weighted pole.

The moment the clew of the sail is clear of the water the sail will swing to the down-

wind position. If the sail is already on the downwind side of you (i.e. with the wind on your back), this is no problem. If it is within 90 degrees or so, you will need to hold the rig so that the clew is just brushing the surface whilst it slides around to the correct position before you can pull it up.

You must have the wind on your back to be able to pull up the sail and set off successfully.

If the board is pointing into the wind, or dead downwind, the sail will want to lie over the tail or nose of the board and you cannot sail off from here. In this situation, you will need to leave the clew dipped in the water and push the board around with your feet until it is pointing in a suitable direction.

In the worst case, the sail is on the 'wrong' side of the board - if the wind is in your face when you are uphauling your rig, you are in trouble! You have two choices - either heave the sail up and swing it over the nose of the board as you hold the uphaul rope, and try again. Or you can, once again, pull it 90% clear of the water and, leaving the clew dipped in, push the board all the way around with your feet until you are facing the right way.

A very useful exercise for early lessons is to practice manoeuvring the board in a full circle whilst keeping the sail stationary relative to the wind.

The safest position in which to hold the rig is with both hands grasping the mast just below the boom. Try to stand up, keep your arms straight, and look ahead. Looking down at your feet for more than a quick glance is counterproductive. The weight of the rig will not produce much power like this, as it naturally orientates itself with the wind direction, though with a breeze it will start to drift gently. If you place one hand on the boom and pull the sail in towards you slightly, you will present the sail to the wind, the airfoil being able to work more efficiently.

The wind in the sail will immediately begin to power the board, and you will start to move. A moving board with some power in the sail is more stable and easier to control than a static board just bobbing around, but the sailor needs to learn how to steer and control that power very quickly or he will soon be drifting into the distance!

Steering

A windsurfer is unlike most other watercraft in that it has no rudder. The steering has to be achieved through moving the different forces acting on the craft in relation to each other, to persuade it to go where we want it to.

When sailing very fast (planing), small changes to the drag on the board, caused by pressure from your feet, or even a single toe, can have a marked effect, and the sail is kept still. (More information on this is given in Chapter 16: Planing.) But initially, when sailing at lower speeds, steering is achieved by moving the rig (i.e. the sail, supported by the mast and boom). How does this work?

The sail is always trying to force the board

in the direction of the wind. If the board is pointing across the wind this is primarily a sideways force.

The sail forms an airfoil and generates power over most of its surface, but the strongest area is located in the middle of the deepest part of the sail, i.e. slightly above where you are holding the boom. For simplicity, the power can be considered as all acting through a single focal point, often referred to as the 'centre of effort' (C of E). More information on this can be found in Chapter 9: How the Sail Works.

The daggerboard, and, to a lesser extent, the fin, both cause drag under the board, as they resist being pushed sideways through the water. The daggerboard is located almost directly below the centre of effort in normal sailing.

If the rig is moved forwards toward the nose of the board (by leaning the rig forwards), the centre of effort affects the front of the board more than the rear, which is being held back by the lateral resistance from the daggerboard and the fin.

The result is that the board pivots around the centre of the resistance and the nose turns downwind.

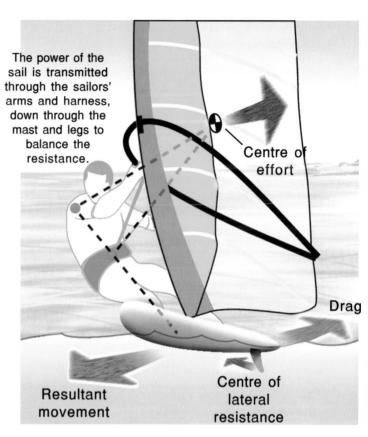

The power of the sail is transmitted through the sailors' arms and harness, down through the mast and legs to balance the resistance.

Centre of effort

Drag

Resultant movement

Centre of lateral resistance

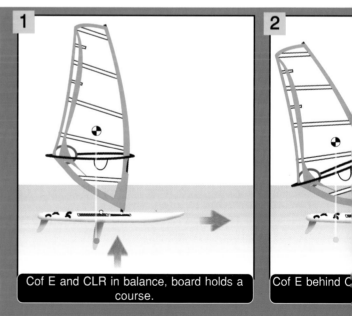

1 Cof E and CLR in balance, board holds a course.

2 Cof E behind C

If the sail is leaned back so that the foot is almost parallel to and nearly touching the board then the centre of effort is located behind the centre of resistance and the opposite happens - the nose pivots back upwind.

The process is exactly like a weather vane - the 'sail' is behind the resistance point, so the vane pivots to face directly upwind. Move the vane in front of the pivot, and the vane would swing to point downwind.

Holding a Course

Simply by leaning the rig backward and forward the sailor can adjust the course of the board. The faster the board is moving, the more effect this has, and the more precise his control. Holding or adjusting your course is the easy part. The fun really starts when you are ready to change direction completely, and sail back to where you came from.

Tacking

This is the term used for turning the board around in an upwind direction, so that the nose briefly points into the wind, before sailing away on the opposite tack (i.e. with the sail on the other side).

Technique: Move your front foot to just forward of the mast foot.

With one hand holding the mast and the other holding the boom near the front, lean the rig back to point up the board into the wind. Unlike adjusting your course, you will now need to hold that position and pull the rig toward your back leg in a sweeping motion that will keep pushing the nose round, right through the eye of the wind.

At the same time, drive the back of the board towards the sail by pushing with your back leg.

You are now at the transition point where the sail is not working and the board is

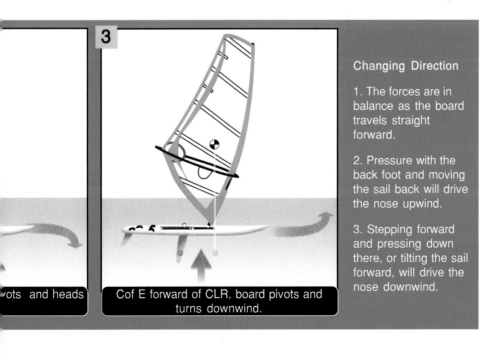

3

Changing Direction

1. The forces are in balance as the board travels straight forward.

2. Pressure with the back foot and moving the sail back will drive the nose upwind.

3. Stepping forward and pressing down there, or tilting the sail forward, will drive the nose downwind.

ots and heads

C of E forward of CLR, board pivots and turns downwind.

Tacking

Rake the rig back & sweep it in towards the back leg

Step smartly around the

Gybing

Rig forward 'The Archer'

Rig raked to outside of turn, body weight
to inside of turn

Switch hands & sheet in to set the new course

slowing or stopping. Any moment now the sail will start to fill from the other side, and if you are still on the same side of the board it will push you off! This is the most likely moment for it to go wrong, so the best advice is to shuffle around to the front of the mast as smartly as you can. You may wish to put both hands on the mast whilst you do this. You are now in a secure position on the other side.

You can now reach over your 'old' back hand to grasp the boom near the clamp, and can move your old front hand back onto the boom; then pull in slightly to power the sail, and away you go!

The key to successful tacking is to be positive and make it happen quickly. Scoop the rig hard, and help the board round by pushing it with your feet; get around the mast quickly and get back under power without delay.

You may find that even after you are around the mast the board is still pointing so far upwind that there is no power to be had. You can encourage the turn further by pushing the clew of the sail away from you for a moment, to pivot the board more quickly. You will fall off quite a bit,

eet & slide the hand up
ards the mast...

Ready to flip the rig & step forwards as
you sail away on the new course

but do not worry - everyone does; it will take a lot of practice to get it spot on.

Of course you need to look at your hands and feet at times to see what is going on, but do not forget that looking forward is a key element of retaining balance. Try to limit yourself to glancing down briefly and looking forward again as soon as possible.

Balance is much easier if there is power in the sail and the board is still moving. Watching experienced sailors tacking, you will soon notice that the sail is powered until the last moment, and the interval between being powered first in one direction and then in the other is very short.

The latest generation of superwide boards make this manoeuvre much easier than used to be the case, but shorter boards (even some of those with high volume) have little of that buoyancy in the nose, and are not suitable for slow tacks, as the nose tends to sink.

Gybing

The gybe is a turn that is made downwind, and instead of you moving around the rig, the rig swings over the nose of the board when changing sides.

Technique: lean the rig forwards until the board is starting to point further downwind. This position has been dubbed 'the Archer', as it is a similar stance to firing a bow into the nose of the board! As the board turns, so you must allow the sail to 'open' to maintain the same angle to the wind.

As the board is pointing dead downwind the sail is at 90% to the board; you may well need to step back slightly and bend

your knees to help control the power of the sail as the board turns. By pushing with your outside foot and leaning the rig towards the outside of the turn you can persuade the board to keep turning so that the tail passes through the eye of the wind. As you feel the sail de-power, you can drop the boom with your back hand and 'flip' the rig onto the new side. A common problem is trying to flip the rig too early. It is a better technique to keep following the wind around with the sail as the board turns, and be sailing 'clew first' for a few moments before flipping the rig.

The actual flip should be a positive action, throw the boom away so that it swings around and slaps into your catching hand ready to go. There is a pause when the rig has changed side, but is still not generating power. You may need to step forward, switch hands on the mast, and 'sheet in' by pulling the boom with your new back hand.

Whilst you are flipping the rig and switching hands, your feet should continue to be pushing the board round onto the new course.

Fast tacking and gybing are covered in more detail in Chapter 13.

Falling Off!

You will fall off many times when learning to windsurf, yet instructors, magazines and holiday brochures often sadly neglect this vital skill!

Falling off tends to slip into three categories: the front door, the back door and the wobbly step off. (You may hear more experienced windsurfers talking about 'catapulting', but that is a more advanced technique requiring special equipment, which is discussed later in this book!)

Whichever method you employ, it is worth noting that you will get completely submerged at times, and can get water up your nose. It can be an unpleasant experience, so you do need to be comfortable in the water.

Going out of the front door

This the situation where the wind is quite strong or gusty and you find you are overpowered - the sensation is as if someone much stronger than you has grabbed your boom on the other side and pulled you sharply towards them. To prevent it you need to automatically sheet out (relax your back arm) and let the sail dump the gust, or you need to step back and squat down to control the power. Once you start walking forward on the board you have lost it, and the sail will pull you straight over into the water on top of it. The golden rule in this situation is to keep both hands on the boom. If you let go you may fall into it and collect a bruise, or at worst damage your sail. Even if you go head over heels onto the top of your sail, it is still better to keep hold if you can.

The good thing about front door exits is that the sail is probably lying on the correct side of the board for an easy uphaul!

Leaving by the back door

This is more likely to be a gentle affair where you are leaning out, and are well committed and the wind dies - you subside backwards into the water. The bad news is that the sail may be on top of your head and you will have to swim out from under it. When you have climbed back on, the sail may need a lot of manoeuvring to get into the correct position to get going again. The good news is that this is great experience for when you are water starting, and many a first water start has begun life as a back door flop followed by a gust that 'resurrected' the sailor from almost certain doom.

The faster and more confident you become with your sailing the more you tend to fall off backwards more than forwards, so this is a positive step! Once again keep hold of the boom as you fall. The reason for this is that a loose rig can fall and give you a nasty crack on the head; if you are holding it this will not happen.

The wobbly step off

This is a bit of a cop-out really, where the sailor drops the rig at the first sign of trouble, then steps off because there is nothing left to hang on to. It mostly happens when you are not trying hard enough! The main advantage is that if you grab the board as you step off you can keep your hair dry!

Stepping off does have an application, however, as the preferred method of avoiding imminent collisions with the beach, other sailors, or obstacles in the water.

The important thing is to do it with style!

Sails & How They Work

The power of the wind is easy to understand - we can all feel the air pushing against us in a strong breeze. When it is pointed downwind, a windsurfer sail will offer resistance to this force and be pushed along just like leaves, or a simple kite.

Thousands of years ago, humans discovered that by angling a sail in a certain way, and shaping their boats with a keel, they could harness this power to make their craft sail across the wind to a greater or a lesser degree (though for quite a while they sensibly kept a few oars handy too!).

Our knowledge has increased hugely over the years, aided in particular by the sci-ence of aerodynamics in the last century. As a result, our sails are now sophisti-cated airfoils that can generate power in a range of winds and (together with the boards) can vector that power so that we can travel considerably faster than the windspeed driving us. We can move in a direction that is predominantly upwind, i.e. towards the pushing force. This is truly remarkable, and is a rare example of getting something for nothing! So how does it work?

How the Sail Works

The loaded sail assumes a curved pro-file, and forms a simple airfoil. The illustration on the next page shows this in cross-section.

The moving air striking the leading edge of the airfoil (the mast) is divided into two streams - one on the windward (up-wind) side and one on the leeward (down-wind) side.

The windward airflow encounters resistance as it is deflected by the sail and creates an area of high pressure. The amount of resistance, and therefore the pressure, varies depending on the angle of the sail to the airflow.

In the illustration the sail is shown at a 'normal' angle of attack (about 20 degrees). If the sail is 'opened' until it is aligned with airflow, which happens when the sailor is holding the mast with both hands, there will be little resistance and very little power. As it is 'closed' or sheeted in, the angle of attack is increased, so the pressure will increase. On a run with the sail at 90 degrees to the wind, the pressure will be very high.

The other airstream travelling over the leeward side is following the curve of the sail, and in doing so it is being 'squeezed' between the curved surface on one side and the rest of the moving airmass, which is trying to carry on in the same direction on the other. The result is similar to squeezing the end of a hosepipe with water flowing out - the narrower space forces the air to accelerate in compensation (the Venturi effect). As the air speeds up, it is 'stretched' over the curved surface, and the pressure reduces.

This reduction of pressure with speed is called the Bernoulli effect, after the physicist who first quantified it. The math involved is detailed in the theorem of the same name (just in case you are interested!).

There is now high pressure on one side of the sail, and a low pressure area on the other. The high is 'pushing' to fill the low pressure area, and the low is 'sucking' the high pressure area. The resulting force is felt as a strong pull at 90 degrees to the maximum camber (curvature) of the airfoil of the sail.

This airfoil action means that the sail is generating power in a slightly forward as well as a sideways direction. This is shown on the diagram as the resultant lateral force.

On the water, if travelling across the wind, the board is designed to offer lateral resistance, (through the daggerboard, fin and rails) in order to balance the sideways component of this power, but the forward component is actively encouraged, by reducing drag as far as possible.

The wind is the engine providing raw power, and the shape of the sail acts to vector this power into a more forward direction. The board then vectors this resultant force into a still more forward direction, and the end result is movement in the direction the board is pointing.

However, there are some limits to this; air is like water, in that it can only change direction smoothly in a gentle curve - force it to make a severe change of direction and it will 'break' and tumble (a waterfall is a good example). The low-pressure area will become a chaotic mix of air rather than a smooth flow, and the aerodynamic force will be lost.

When the sail is moved to a very high angle of attack (sheeted right in on a broad reach, for example), the sail will stall, the airflow becomes chaotic on the leeward side, and power is lost. If the angle

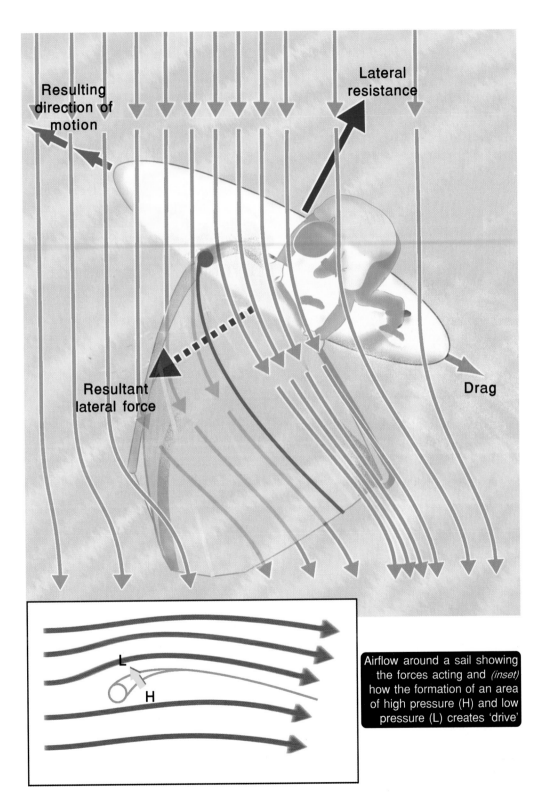

Resulting
direction of
motion

Lateral
resistance

Resultant
lateral force

Drag

L

H

Airflow around a sail showing
the forces acting and *(inset)*
how the formation of an area
of high pressure (H) and low
pressure (L) creates 'drive'

of attack is too low (sail sheeted out on an upwind course) then, although the airfoil will work, it will generate less power than if it were sheeted in to the optimum angle.

Aerodynamically speaking, then, the worst case scenarios are when pointing directly upwind or downwind. When upwind, the sail is not working at all and generates no power. Unless you have deliberately stopped for a chat, a rest, or to adjust your kit, this is a bad situation to be in, so when tacking, it is a good idea to get through the directly upwind sector or 'no-go zone' as quickly as possible.

Because the rig is just a dead weight, and you soon stop moving, the board can feel very unstable, too, in this situation.

Dead downwind is slightly different - opening the sail to present maximum area to the wind you stall the airfoil and lose all your 'sucking' force, which can be well over half the normal power of the sail. However, at the same time you are massively increasing the 'pushing' force with a very large high-pressure area. In practice, this means that if you are moving along well and turn directly downwind, the power is likely to decrease overall, and you will slow down.

However, if you are moving very slowly with the sail is not working effectively, and you turn downwind and get the full benefit of the high pressure, you may feel a sudden surge of power and struggle to control it.

Available power is a function of using the sail efficiently, but it is also largely determined by the size of the sail you have chosen. On the subject of size, this is an area that many sailors are wary of..

Choosing Sail Size

Your choice of sail size depends on many factors. Out-and-out racers will choose the largest sail they can hold down for maximum possible power, but power is useless without control, and the board, fin, and above all the sailor must be capable of handling the chosen sail! The best advice is to ask what others are using and honestly assess your own capabilities before choosing. You do need to be confident enough to choose a sail big enough to make the most of the conditions, but if you are grossly overpowered your sailing experience will not be much fun. Heavier and stronger sailors can handle larger sails, and wide boards with big fins can also handle bigger sails than low volume boards.

Until you are pretty experienced, as a general rule it is better to be underpowered and have to come in to change up a size, than be overpowered and have to come in to change down!

Sail design is quite a subtle art, and there are other, less obvious, features that are important in a modern sail.

Sail Design

The airfoil section chosen is critical to the power a sail can produce, and by using different camber (curvature) profiles the sail can be varied between high power (steeply cambered) or with a wider useable range (lower camber) of shapes. This is determined to some extent by the battens used; an effective way to help create a steep camber toward the leading edge of the sail is to use a small device called a camber inducer (surprisingly enough).

A camber inducer (or 'cam' for short) uses

The high-tenacity Dacron luff tube is cut in a curve to match the stiffness & curve of the mast

Many sails feature tuning marks to help identify the correct tensioning.

Adjustable head batten tension minimises flutter.

Roller cams are fitted to the batten ends in race oriented sails.

Mini battens are made of layers of glassfibre or TriX and prevent the sail fluttering in the loose roach area.

Batten pockets are fitted with tension adjusters and anti-scuff protection.

Different weights of TriX laminate are used in areas of high stress.

Two clew options for adjustable height.

The tack area is protected by a padded sleeve.

The tack has either a cringle (metal grommet) to accept a pulley hook or is fitted with its own trim device.

Reinforced foot to minimise wear from the board.

Sail anatomy

73

Sail twist

These devices require more work from the sailmaker, and add somewhat to the rigging hassles and weight of a sail, but they do increase the power available. For these reasons, they are most commonly found on race sails, which may feature as many as seven cams.

Rotational sails generate only slightly less overall power and tend to use airfoil sections that have the maximum camber point a little further back. These are less fussy about perfect tuning and angle of attack, so they give a wider 'powerband' and are a bit lighter and easier to rig. Some beginner sails and wave orientated sails are non-rotational and are designed primarily for ease of handling and stability rather than power.

The angle of attack, and therefore the power output of a sail, is not a constant across a whole sail. A sail is always twisted to some extent, with the head operating at a lower angle than the lower part. This difference in angle is known as twist or 'washout' in aerodynamic terms.

Some twist is cut into the sail, but it is primarily controlled by mast stiffness. It is necessary for a couple of reasons.

The first is aerodynamic; the airstreams at different pressures are almost matched by the time they meet at the head of the sail and this reduces drag. If this were not the case there would be a much larger tip vortex (see illustration overleaf), and the sail may be slowed down. The prime purpose of the roached area of the leech is to release power in a controlled manner.

The second is practical; a sailor must handle the sail, and if the pressure difference were very strong all the way up the sail, the centre of effort would be lo-

the compression of the batten to hold the sail in a set or loaded shape, even if there is no wind in the sail.

This means that such a sail will use even the smallest breath of wind, and because the twist and airfoil shape is better controlled, may allow the sail to point upwind a little further before it loses power.

cated much higher up. In fact as the power increases the centre of effort effectively moves down, making it easier for the sailor to handle. An untwisted sail would be much more powerful, but would be almost impossible to control.

If more power is needed, a better solution is to use a larger sail.

There is potentially a very big vortex at the foot of the sail, and this is one reason that sails are rigged to sit as close as practical to the board, interrupting the migration of pressure (and therefore power) around the bottom edge. When planing, experienced sailors will rake the rig back until the foot of the sail is virtually touching the board to seal this gap com-

Airflow around a moving sail

pletely (a technique known as 'closing the slot'). This ensures that the foil is operating at maximum efficiency.

Sailors can also alter the camber and the amount of twist in their sails by increasing or decreasing downhaul and outhaul. A very tight, flat sail has the camber reduced, and will generate a bit less power; the tension between the clew and the head of the mast will also allow the roached section of sail to 'float' more easily, and increase the washout, further reducing power. Many sailors will alter the tuning of their sail in this way to cater for

changing conditions. However, if you are sailing in strong winds, and turn downwind with such a sail, the power surge will be very noticeable!

There is no substitute for choosing the correct size sail!

The planform (flat shape) of the sail has gradually evolved over the years - a noticeable feature being the design of the tip, which has moved from a pointed to a more 'square' shape. The tip design is primarily concerned with minimising drag and allowing the airstreams on each side of the sail to rejoin without too much drama. This shape maximises twist, and helps de-power the sail in gusts but retain power in lulls.

Drag reduction has also driven the 'cleaning up' of sails by removing external batten adjusters and protruding masts etc. The shape of the foot varies from high-cut sails that are required for radical manoeuvring in waves, to low-cut shapes that mirror the board profile, allowing closing the slot effectively in race sails.

The luff-tube is the fabric tube into which the mast is slotted. A narrow luff-tube is found on freeride and wave sails, and a broader one on more race-orientated sails. A narrow tube is light and does not trap much water, but a broader one acts as a fairing to the mast and is more efficient in an aerodynamic sense; it also gives a bit of room to locate any camber inducers.

Sail Materials

The favoured material for many sails is extruded polyester film. Unlike woven fabric, it is equally stable in all directions, you can see through it (always an advantage) and it is easily worked. A single layer of this material is known as monofilm. On the downside, it does age quite quickly and can easily be scratched by sand and even by the tiny salt crystals that precipitate out of drying seawater. It is tough, but once penetrated, the lack of a woven structure means that a split can easily spread right across a sail.

Monofilm loses about 50% of its structural strength after about 300 hours of direct sunlight.

Depending how it is stored and used, the life expectancy can range from one hard season in a school in Egypt to 6 or 7 years occasional use in the UK!

Dacron fabric is used for the luff-tube and stress areas like sail batten pockets. Unlike monofilm, it is very flexible and resistant to abrasion. It takes seams well and can be dyed any colour. Dacron sails are a rarer sight these days, but they do make very durable and quiet sails!

In stressed sail panels or on sails expected to take some hammer, the monofilm is usually replaced with a reinforced laminate.

Laminates are constructed by sandwiching a scrim (mesh) of a tougher material between two layers of monofilm. The

scrim substrate is composed of a tough light material such as super Aramid (often known by DuPont's trade name of Kevlar), Polyester, or Dyneema (known as Spectra in the USA).

These 3-layer laminates are slightly heavier, a bit stiffer, and more expensive, but are extremely durable.

Many sails feature a softer and slightly stretchier central panel, usually of optically clear PVC. This looks like monofilm, but is slightly different in its properties. Its increased elasticity helps absorb impacts, and allows it to recover its shape when dented or stretched; - an important feature, as this the area you are likely to hit when you fall into the sail.

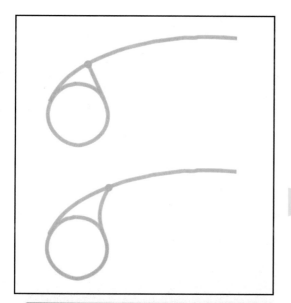

(Top) Rotational sail; where the batten end rotates or flips around the mast (this may be aided by cams on race sails) and *(Bottom)* Non-rotational sail; where the batten end remains clear of the mast

The Quiver

Of course all sailors all want lightweight, tough, easy rig, inexpensive, super-fast and very tolerant sails! And on the whole they get a pretty good selection; there are any number of rotational or non-rotational sails for easy use, and hybrid sails with one, two, or three cams, or sails featuring some freeride and some race sail or wave riding features.

Apart from real specialist applications, most of them do most things pretty well!

However, you do need a choice of sizes (a quiver of sails). Most new sailors will start with a medium sized freeride sail. For an adult male this is likely to be in the 5 to 6.5m. range. For sailing in lighter winds, the next purchase is likely to be 7 to 7.5m. or so - by the time you are looking at this sized sail, you may wish to consider a couple of cams to boost your performance a bit; and finally, a smaller sail of perhaps 4 to 5m. for those howling days. Of course this all depends on your prevailing local sailing conditions and style!

A moderately sized freeride (rotational) sail, combined with a good wind, is the easiest choice for new manoeuvres such as learning to waterstart or carve gybe.

Tuning

There are two major adjustments that you can make to the sail - outhaul and downhaul. The outhaul on most modern sails is sensitive to change, but fortunately it is easy to adjust and needs very little power. In fact many sails will be perfectly happy with no outhaul pressure at all - simply a connection of the clew to the boom.

Telescopic boom and sail with 3 clew height options

Downhaul pulley hook detail

If the outhaul is too slack, the sail will show vertical wrinkles: if too tight, it will show wrinkles pointing at the clew.

In light wind situations, the sail can be encouraged to adopt a fuller and more cambered shape by using 'negative outhaul': this is the situation when the distance from the mast to the clew of the sail is longer than from the mast to the inside of the boom end. The sail has no tension from the clew until it has cambered in a deeper curve than usual.

The downhaul is the major adjustment and tuning mechanism. As you pull down, the mast is bent into a curve. This curve is determined by the stiffness of the mast and the pressure lines of the sail (which too much outhaul will also affect).

The more downhaul, the more the leech is opened, allowing a softer upper trailing edge, and the more the camber of the sail is flattened (moving the centre of effort back and reducing the power).

New sails will come with a manual suggesting the range of tuning available. But it is worth noting that this will not be too helpful if the mast is the wrong stiffness for that sail.

Note: As you alter the downhaul, so the outhaul is affected, and vice-versa. It is not uncommon to see sailors moving from one point to the other and back again, in an attempt to get the balance just right.

Masts come in stock sizes - 430cm; 460cm; 490cm, etc. However, not all sails have a luff that fits exactly to this length. Mast extensions can be added, but to get a precise fit on a longer mast most sails smaller than around 6.0m. will have an adjustable head strap, which allows the sail to be fitted with the foot at the bottom of the mast.

Most adjustable heads are simple straps and buckles. The cap that actually fits over the mast is either moulded plastic, or webbing.

Sail and Rigging Troubleshooting

Sail instability and poor rotation is most commonly caused by not enough downhaul, if in doubt give it an extra heave!

If the cams are difficult to get on the mast, make sure that the sail has no downhaul tension but is outhauled fully before snapping the cam on.

If the battens are reluctant to flip through, the problem may be that the cam bearing battens are too compressed. Try releasing a little batten tension. However the most common problem is that the cam is over-rotated, and you need more downhaul, and possibly more outhaul.

This is often identified when the battens are buckled into a "S" shape before popping through.

(Right) Rig tuned with lots of downhaul, for strong conditions. Note the curve of the mast and the very loose roached area.   *(Left)* The same rig with less downhaul, the mast is straighter and the sail roach is tighter.

The Board & How it Works

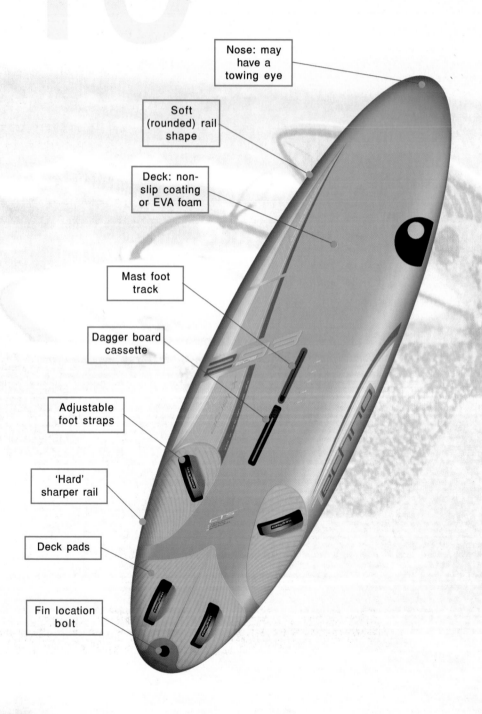

Nose: may have a towing eye

Soft (rounded) rail shape

Deck: non-slip coating or EVA foam

Mast foot track

Dagger board cassette

Adjustable foot straps

'Hard' sharper rail

Deck pads

Fin location bolt

At first glance, a windsurf board is simply a floating plank, but when you see how much they cost, you realise there must be more to it than that (and there is!). In fact, each board is a subtle blend of design features, and even a slight change in the curve of the undersurface, the profile of a rail, or the position of a fin can have a dramatic impact on its performance and handling.

Size and Volume

The board does of course need to float, and exactly how "floaty" it is an important consideration. Each litre of volume can support 1kg. Therefore a sailor weighing (say) 80kg for example, and with a board and rig adding a further 15kg will need 95litres of volume just to avoid sinking.

Some wave boards, which are designed to cut though chop, slash radical turns up the face of a wave, and get big air in jumps, have a volume of perhaps 80 litres, or even less.

The weight of most riders and rigs will make them sink if they slow down, and they must be beach or water started.

A modern beginner's board may have in excess of 200 litres of volume - plenty for a heavier sailor to stroll around on the deck!

Because a very low volume board is of little use if the wind drops, all boards designed for the beginner or recreational sailor tend to be at least 120 litres.

'Freerace' hybrid board 110 -130 ltr

Wave board <100 ltr

'Formula' race board 200 ltr +

'Freeride' board with dagger 160 ltr +

Superwide beginners board 200 ltr +

Although anyone can sail any sized board in the right conditions, it is becoming more common for manufacturers to offer a range of sizes in each model, so that you can match your body weight and board volume more accurately.

Shape

A shorter, broader shape will lift out of the water onto the plane more easily, so this has been taken to its logical conclusion with the new breed of superwide boards, which are generally around 1m in width. They offer a very stable platform for the new sailor, and the evenly distributed volume means that it easy to step around the mast without sinking the nose.

This type of board has quickly gained popularity since about 2001; it is making the sport much more accessible, and, to some extent, changing the nature of windsurfing by making many early goals achievable much more quickly.

At the other end of the scale are the 'speed needles' and wave boards. These feature a much narrower shape, designed to be much more manoeuvrable and manageable in stronger winds and rougher seas.

The outline of a board gives a good indication of its handling characteristics.

Straight or parallel edges (rails) indicate good directional stability and upwind ability.

Because a straight edge will produce less drag, these boards will be faster than the very rounded ones.

More curved rails give a 'looser' feel, as they allow the board to be turned more easily and be pivoted more tightly without 'stalling' it and losing speed.

Most sailors who have reached the planing stage and are buying their own kit, choose a freeride board, which is a compromise of these features. A broader tail area, thick enough to give sufficient volume for uphauling, but a thinner, narrower nose. Some freeride boards feature a dagger board and others do not.

This classic teardrop shape has really now taken over completely from the old long boards, which used to be the only alternative to the short "sinkers" used by experienced water-starters. However, they are not quite as stable as very wide boards, nor will they have the top end speed of a short narrow board, or the manoeuvrability of a wave board.

Because of the durability of the old blow-moulded long boards of 320cm and more, it is likely that they will still be giving service at many training centres for some years.

There are a wide variety of boards available. Below is a brief introduction to the major types, though more and more designs are actually a crossover of types.

Formula boards

Formula boards are primarily the most modern race boards - very wide and short, they look very like the newest beginner models. They're designed for planing as soon as possible on both upwind and downwind courses, and for carrying massive sails.

Recreational short boards

This covers a large family of models; essentially they are all aimed at planing conditions, and they vary between wide flat early planers that are good in light winds to those more at home slashing around in chop and stronger winds with smaller sails.

This group can be subdivided into three broad categories:

Freeride boards

This is the biggest group, and caters for the largest portion of the sailing activity at most venues - blasting around as fast as possible in a range of conditions.

Typically quite high volume at 120-170 litres, and usually with no daggerboard, these are the best choice as a second board once you are planing, or even as a first board, if you are capable and ambitious.

Wave boards

These are the smallest, lowest volume, most manoeuvrable and the trickiest to master for an inexperienced sailor. However, if your thing is playing in big waves and getting big air, these are the weapons you need! Most experienced coastal sailors will have a wave board stashed away for those epic days.

Freestyle boards

This is a tough group to define. Freestyle used to mean doing various cool stunts like helicopter tacks and sailing backwinded, requiring a pretty stable platform. But the massive steps forward in the standard of freestyle in just a couple of years have changed it into a very technical discipline, in which huge airs and loops, etc., are now the accepted standard. As a result, the boards are becoming close cousins of the dedicated wave boards to reflect this. 'Freestyle' and 'freeride', are easy to confuse, but they are, in fact, diverging quickly. A modern board described as 'freestyle' is likely to be unsuitable for an inexperienced sailor. *NB: None of them are actually free, of course!*

Race Boards

Although any boards can be raced, the term is usually applied to the specialist 375 racing long boards. Designed to be as fast as possible when not planing, and with unrivalled upwind performance, they are really only of interest to dedicated class racers.

Board Anatomy

The diagram overleaf shows the construction of a modern board.

Boards are constructed in a variety of ways. Virtually all of them are based on a core of hard, low-density expanded polystyrene foam, which has millions of air bubbles in it, giving good buoyancy. The core is strengthened with the inclusion of one or more 'stringers'- thin lengthwise layers of stronger material, like wood or glass-fibre.

This is encased in a rigid skin of strong waterproof material. The cheapest and toughest method is blow-moulding, using a plastic skin that can be easily mass-produced.

This method is excellent for a beginner board, as the skin is very resistant to knocks; though if it is damaged it may be difficult to repair. Blow-moulded boards are relatively heavy.

It is possible to construct a lighter board by using an outer skin of thin fibreglass.

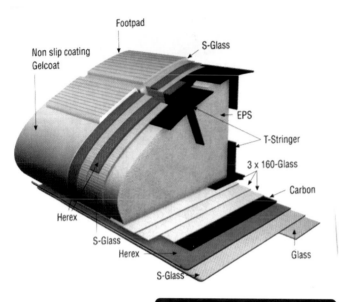

Board construction *(Pic: Gun Sails)*

Labels: Footpad, Non slip coating Gelcoat, S-Glass, EPS, T-Stringer, 3 x 160-Glass, Carbon, Herex, S-Glass, Herex, Glass, S-Glass

This is also inexpensive, but is more fragile. The reduced strength of the skin means that the 'stringers' in the core are critical for strength. It is also easy to effect minor repairs, which is just as well, as it is quite possible to damage the nose of one of these boards by whacking it with your boom if you wipe out at speed.

Some more expensive boards use carbon fibre, herex or other composite materials for the layers of the skin, plus a sandwich of different foam materials to give maximum rigidity and lightness. All these finish the job with a layer of coloured resin, which can incorporate the all-important board graphics!

Wood is a material that is also staging a comeback. Though slightly more expensive to manufacture than moulded materials, the wood-and-foam-laminate boards are proving a popular and effective choice.

Bottom surface

The underside of the board is as slippery as possible; the usual cross-section of a recreational board is now almost perfectly flat, though this has not always been the case. Concave or double concave hulls have been used at various times, and in recent times certain new formula boards have again utilised the multi-hull approach, the hydrodynamics can get quite complex, but essentially the idea of this is to try and "tunnel" the water-flow and

A nice new woody - a work or art!

Wave board showing the 'V' profile of the rear section *(Photo: Bic)*

promote early planing. Channelled undersurfaces can also help the fin provide lateral resistance and balance the large forces generated by carrying big sails in strong winds.

Many boards, particularly long boards and wave boards, use a tapered 'V' section toward the back of the board; this increases stability in rough water by minimising the 'slapping' as the board deals with chop. On wave boards the V also serves to help the manoeuvrability by keeping one side flatter as the board is banked, and the angle of the water escaping from the inside rail is less radical, so may generate less turbulence and drag than a more deeply submerged edge. An important purpose of the V is to initiate the division of the water flow around the fin and minimise the turbulent flow and ventilation (bubbles) caused by the fin and board moving through the water.

Board shaping is a science as well as an art!

Freestyle board designs have also experimented with grooves and channels, sometimes known as phazers - these are a

Marco Copello , board shaper; at work
(Photo: Gun)

(Left) Freestyle board, showing Undersurface channelling and *(right)* a double concave undersurface - this is a Starboard Hypersonic.

crossover from surf and wake-board technology, and help to maintain a degree of directional control when sailing backwards and to minimise the size of fin required.

Other possible undersurface shapes, like concave sections or stepped designs, have all been tried.

Rocker

When looked at in profile, the curve in the bottom surface is quite clear; this curve, or 'rocker' is designed to keep the nose from being buried in every bit of swell and to help lift the board onto the plane. On a wave board that may be pitched up a wave face, then dropped down the other side, a deep rocker curve is a major advantage. Of course, it also presents a steeper angle to any water it hits, so it reduces the top speed in most sailing where the surface is rippled or choppy.

Many boards also feature some curve in the tail area;

This is commonly seen on modern freestyle boards that are designed for manoeuvres that may involve sailing or landing a jump tail first!

The most pronounced curve is found on wave boards, where it is important that this small area is in contact with the water for as long as possible to allow sharp manoeuvres, when a flatter board may have

Gentle rocker of a freeride bo

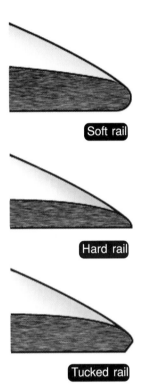

Soft rail

Hard rail

Tucked rail

Hard or sharp rail towards the rear

Tucked rails

a bigger area in contact or have bounced clear altogether.

Rails

The rails (edges) of the board have a different shape, depending on their function.

Toward the front of the board they are rounded in section (soft); this helps the water adhere to the rail and minimises turbulence and drag. Towards the tail of the board the rails become sharper (hard), allowing the water to break away more easily and aiding acceleration and handling when the board is planing. Theoretically, hard rails have the advantage, particularly for upwind performance (and are found on long race boards throughout their length), but they are very 'on-off' in nature, (hence the name) and a softer rail minimises the jerkiness caused when a hard rail catches and releases the water - a situation that occurs continuously in the forward section of the board until it is planing at full bore (when, of course, the front rails are clear, so it does not matter).

The rounded top and sharp bottom pro-

different designers have arrived at a variety of solutions and shapes, from pin tails to squared-off ends.

Some dedicated wave boards, built specifically for particular conditions, use an asymmetric shape with a differently shaped tail on each side. Some freestyle boards feature "scooped" duck-tail designs to help with sliding and sailing backwards and reducing the tail catching. This type of design feature is really only important to sailors who are performing Vulcans and similar tricks on a regular basis.

file of the tucked rail combine these characteristics, acting as a normal rail until the board lifts out of the water, when it starts to release from the bottom, aiding early planing.

Tail

The design of the tail area is very important, as this is the only part of the board (together with the fin) that is in the water when you are fully planing. The shape must allow the water to escape without too much drag. This is an area where

Deck

The top surface of the board is known as the deck, and is generally coated in a non-slip material of some type. On beginners' boards where the sailor is likely to spend a good deal of time clambering back on to up-haul, the favoured material is hi-density EVA foam bonded to the deck. This is very comfortable, and although it is easily scratched and scraped, it is very effective and very wet-suit- (and skin) friendly.

Other boards use a granular finish that feels like sandpaper, or sharkskin (we are reliably informed!);

Deck pads

this offers excellent friction, even underwater, and is a big advantage when moving fast and your feet could easily slip.

It chews up the skin on your forearms and knees if you are scrambling on repeatedly, or, even worse, it wears holes in the knees of your nice new wetsuit! However, once you are waterstarting, it is definitely advantageous to have this kind of non -slip surface.

On all but the oldest training boards, the areas immediately around your footstraps will feature a deck pad of rubber matting or ribbed cushioning material. This helps to minimise the impact damage of your heels when bouncing through chop at speed or landing a big jump! It also reduces wear on the soles of your feet or boots.

Mast track

In early board designs the mast position could be moved fore and aft in its track by using a foot pedal, but virtually all modern boards now feature a short mast track slot which requires the position to be set before each session.

Most modern boards should have the deck plate fixed into the mast track at around 135cm from the tail. (This will often be marked on the deck next to the track).

Further forward than this may be useful to maintain mast-foot pressure, and further back if at high speeds the rig cannot be raked back far enough, but for most sailors who are not racing the "normal" 135cm position is generally a good option.

Daggerboards

On boards fitted with a daggerboard, the pedal or lever to operate it is located just behind the mast track. Moving the pedal backwards with your instep rotates the daggerboard down into the vertical position. This gives maximum lateral resistance for sailing upwind, and adds stability to the board.

At low speeds it also acts as a pivot point to help you turn.

Rotating the pedal forward retracts the dagger into a recess in the board. This reduces the drag and allows better board acceleration. It also allows gybing to be executed much more quickly at speed, as the board pivots around the fin only.

Some boards have no dagger but feature a removable central fin; this cleans up the deck area, and is no doubt easier to manufacture. In the early days, the fin is left on and is removed when the sailor is ready to get planing.

This is great for early training, and fine when you are blasting around OK. It is when you are in that critical in-between stage that a problem can arise....the

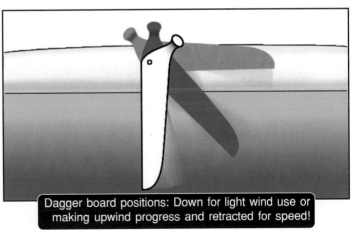

Dagger board positions: Down for light wind use or making upwind progress and retracted for speed!

problem being that you need to be on the beach, and have a screwdriver handy to make the transition.

Unfortunately, there is the fairly common situation that arises at some venues, of being out in marginal planing conditions, when at times you need to make maximum progress upwind and at other times want maximum speed. In this case the lack of flexibility of a fixed centre fin can be an annoyance.

The Fin

The fin is a vital component in balancing the power generated by the sail. When planing with no daggerboard, it is the focus of all the lateral resistance.

The size and shape is important in determining the upwind performance, and as the pivot point for tacks and gybes, it is also critical to the handling of the board.

The fin acts in a very similar manner to

(1) Wave fin
(2) Freeride fin *(Bicsport)*
(3) Speed fin
(4) Weed fin *(Gun)*
(5) Freestyle fin
(6) Slalom fin

the sail, in that the waterflow generates a high pressure area on one side and a low pressure area on the other. When working hard at speed, the fin creates lift , and this helps push the tail of the board higher out of the water. At full speed, perhaps one third of the area in contact with the water is accounted for by the fin, and so its contribution is critical.

Because fins are under such high pressures, but at the same time need to be as thin as possible to minimise drag in a forward direction, they are made of very tough materials, generally glass or carbon fibre, to reduce flexing and the risk of snapping. When the stage of being concerned with maximising the performance of the board is reached, the fin choice comes under close scrutiny, and the size and shape can be altered to match the sail size and the sailing conditions, with different variations being available for slalom, wave, or freeriding use.

The basic variations are:

- Large deep fin with a big area, to balance large boards carrying big sails. These help the upwind performance especially in lighter winds. The more vertical the shape the more speed orientated the fin.

- A smaller and more swept fins are for small agile wave boards. Upwind performance is less important than strength and quick turning.

- Fins for freeride use are a compromise between these two extremes

There also more specialised fin styles: Freestyle fins are also very short as the boards are small, and they need to be easy to get clear of the water, but they must also generate good resitance when needed, and so the blunt triangle shape has developed. Slalom fins are straight and sharp for speed, but the boards are much smaller and so they are scaled down from the huge formula fins. The most specialised of all is the weed fin, raked at an angle to shed vegetation in areas prone to floating weed.

There are very many variations on these basic themes, and experienced sailors will swap their fin to suit their sail size or the prevailing conditions.

Fins are attached by slotting into a hard plastic cassette inset into the board. Like deck-plates, finboxes are not all the same!

The commonest systems are:

- The 'Tuttle box'(this uses two bolts, and is found only on large course racing boards).

- Single bolt-through systems - the 'Power box' (used by Mistral and F2) and 'Trim box'(Bic, Fanatic) .

- The Conic box, unique to Tiga.

- Some wave boards still use the 'Classic box' system.

If buying a new fin (or board) ensure you know which type you need!

All fins are prone to damage if grounded, and care must be taken to keep them sharp and clean. A fin cover is a good idea for car-top transport, and they should be removed if travelling long distances or storing your board for long periods.

How the Board Works

In the previous chapter, the effect of the forces generated by the sail and the daggerboard and fin to produce movement in the desired direction was examined. But once moving, how does the board operate? At low speeds it is simply a very small boat, pushing its way through the water. At a certain speed the board begins to plane.

Planing has been mentioned many times already and is the primary goal of all new sailors. So what exactly is planing?

Planing

When moving fast over the water the board overtakes and 'surfs' its own bow-wave in a process known as planing. Whilst a stationary or slow moving board will not support much weight, and may even sink when a sailor stands on it, a planing board actually generates lift as it moves along, and the faster it goes, the more weight it can support. (In fact, as long as the angle of attack is correct,

the lift a board produces is proportional to the speed of the board squared.) So the faster you are going, the less surface you need to support you.

Planing occurs when the board is moving fast, and generates more and more lift - as it rises, so the stagnation point moves backwards along the bottom surface. At this point the board needs to be flattened to avoid dragging the tail. As the stagnation point moves back behind the centre of gravity, the board will start to skim over its own pressure wave.

The angle of attack mentioned is the angle of the lower surface of the board with the water; this varies with the amount of 'rocker', or curve, which the designer has built into the board, but is principally a function of the sailor's weight distribution. Too much pressure transmitted through the back foot, or not enough through the mastfoot, and you can sink the tail and reduce the efficiency quite dramatically.

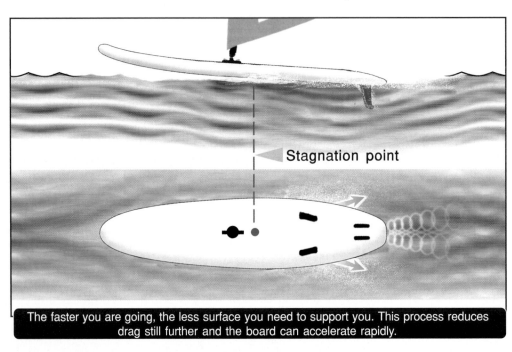

Stagnation point

The faster you are going, the less surface you need to support you. This process reduces drag still further and the board can accelerate rapidly.

Once the board is planing, the drag reduces significantly, and the power required to maintain it is therefore noticeably less. The faster the board is travelling, the smaller the area in contact with the water and the lower the drag.

It is in this state that the board, fin and sail are all operating as a balanced system, and the windsurfer paradoxically feels both more stable and more alive under your feet.

Tuning

The forces are finely balanced in a planing board, and all the action is happening right below your feet. By a subtle shift in stance, altering the pressure pattern of your feet and the mast foot, you can control the board's behaviour. Unlike at slower speeds the key to small adjustments is to keep the rig still; steering is done primarily with your feet.

Press with the toes on the inside (leeward) rail and the board swings downwind - press with the heels on the windward rail and it heads up again. The faster you are moving and the further back under your feet the balance point is, the more sensitive the board will become. It is not uncommon for inexperienced sailors, travelling fast and hitting chop, to start weaving as they over-steer. The faster you go the more you need to relax!

In the picture overleaf, Julien is still in the same position relative to the board, sail and fin, but by applying pressure with his right foot on the inside (leeward) rail the whole thing has banked over at 50 degrees or so and is carving around a nice turn.

Carve gybing is discussed in Chapter 21.

Planing! The board feels stable but more alive under your feet.

Photo: Bic

Changing Direction

Faster Tacking.

The first attempts at turning the board through the wind are often slow, unstable and rather wobbly affairs. There is not much that can be done about the lack of stability in this situation, but we can improve matters by making the whole process a lot faster. The key to success is moving from a stable position with a loaded sail and a solid boom to hold onto on the entry course, to the same situation on the exit course, with a minimum of time spent in between.

With this as the goal it is clear that the tack should be a quick and dynamic manoeuvre. To set up a quick tack, the optimum entry should be from a good forward speed, with the rig raked back

and sheeted in, so that the sail foot is very close to the shin of the back leg. Push hard with the back leg at the same time to send the tail of the board around to meet the sail, which should be brought well past the centre line of the board.

As the sail is coming around and the board pivots, step sharply around the mast with the front foot - if the foot can be placed so that the toes are pointing almost back down the board on the other side this will reduce the number of steps required.

As the board passes through the wind and onto the new course, quickly step up with your back foot, and immediately place your old front foot in the new back foot position on the new side. This is the

The fast tack

most unstable point, but if you can cross your hands to get a grip on the new side of the boom, and grab it with the new back hand, you can immediately tilt the rig forwards to catch the wind and load the sail on the new side.

In the pictures below the sailor is sweeping the rig hard, so that the sail-foot is touching his back leg; this is pushing the nose through the wind. He is stepping right round the mast so that his toes are behind the mast foot on the other side.

In the second shot he has nipped quickly around the mast, but the 125-litre board is mostly submerged with his 95kg. weight close to the mast foot. Note the rig is tilted well forward.

In picture three he has pushed the board around onto the new course and has sheeted in hard. He has stepped back and squatted to help control the surge of power as the rig catches the wind again. A few moments later he was hooked in and planing away on the new course.

With some skill and practice you will find that it is possible to complete this dance and be hanging onto a loaded sail again

in less time than it takes to fall off backwards! A common variation is grasp the mast with one hand as you tack.

The fast tack is a vital skill on most 'teardrop' shaped boards (even those with considerable volume), as it tends to all be located towards the back of the board and standing still in front of the mast is no longer an available option. The smaller the board, the faster the tack required to avoid sinking the nose, and many low-volume board sailors tend to rely almost exclusively on gybing.

Gybing ('Jibing' in the U.S.)

The gybe can be separated into three overlapping categories:

The basic beginner's gybe, used in light winds, where the board remains flat in the water and is steered all the way around by a combination of sail position and foot pressure.

The 'flare' gybe, where the sailor sinks the tail of the board and pivots it around the fin, and the carve gybe, which is initiated from a planing board and will (hopefully) maintain the board on the

plane all the way through the turn.

The most basic light wind gybe is covered in the "basic control" chapter, this section deals with progressing from the basic gybe to the flare gybe, this is a non-planing gybe used in light to moderate winds.

Before attempting a flare gybe the daggerboard should be retracted.

The basic gybe is modified and speeded up by stepping well back on the board with both feet and squatting quite low as the sail opens. This is essential if there is a moderate wind, because there will be a surge of power that you need to control. Stay too far forward or upright, and the sail will pull you over the front of the board. By stepping back you will find that the tail of the board starts to sink.

This is a good thing, as by lifting the front of the board from the water you can pivot it around much more easily. (Leaning the sail out to one side causes the 'shortened' board to screw around neatly.) This type of pivoted turn is known as a 'flare gybe', or if performed at carving

This sailor has sunk the tail, the board is "flaring" up with the nose high and he can easily pivot the short waterline around the fin.

speed is a Slam Gybe.

This is a technique that you will use a great deal as you are learning and it is worth spending a lot of time practising.

As you feel the tail is sinking, the temptation is to step forwards again, which is fine if the board is already turned. However, if you stiffen your arms and lean forward (hoisting some of your weight from your feet) and press the mast foot back down, you will find that, with practice, you can flatten or sink the tail with quite small adjustments of weight.

(A very good exercise to perfect this control is to try sailing downwind for a while with your feet submerged.)

As you become used to this tail sinking, you will find that leaning the rig to one side to pivot the board becomes more and more effective as the boards wetted area is shortened. With a good breeze (and practice!), you can sink the tail over your ankles and achieve a very tight change of course.

As the board comes onto the new heading you must step sharply forwards again to resume your normal sailing position. It is possible to carry on sailing clew-first for a few moments before choosing a moment to flip the rig. Avoid flipping the rig too early - wait until you are on your new course.

As the wind strength increases, you will find the sail becomes rather less stable in the clew- first position and you will need to get the nose well round onto the new course and flip the rig as soon as you step forward.

To achieve a good rig flip, ensure your front hand is positioned well forward, close to the clamp. When you choose your moment, throw the rig away with your back hand so that it comes right around onto the new side in one smooth sweep, and reach over your wrist with the old back hand to grasp the boom on the new side. This should be a strong, confident movement. Many a gybe comes apart because of uncommitted actions.

It may not look too cool to start with, but weaving your way downwind flare gybing from one side to the other is a brilliant way to master control of the board, and will pay dividends later.

The next stage - 'carve gybing' - is covered in Chapter 21.

Sailing With Others

Windsurfing is a leisure activity, and because it is a sport it is perhaps too easy to forget that you are subject to the same rules and laws as all other vessels, and you do have responsibilities to other water users.

By far the most significant chance of collision for windsurfers is with other windsurfers, but a growing group who can take up a lot of space are the kitesurfers, who require very similar conditions and locations. (In fact kitesurfers are very often the same people, who simply choose their weapon according to conditions! This is good from the point of view that windsurfers will be aware of what a kitesurfer is and what they are capable of, but bad in that it means segregation is sometimes not a realistic option.)

There are plenty of other water users, ranging from swimmers to ferries, that we may need to avoid.

To minimise conflict there are a few common sense rulers that can help us all.

■ Try and use an area separate to other water users, particularly when you are a beginner and will be likely to drop the sail. Floating around in the entrance to

Beaches can be busy places!

the local harbour will not impress other sailors.

- Keep a good lookout. This may sound obvious, but holding a mental picture of the other water users that you update every few seconds by scanning the area will help you anticipate conflicts in plenty of time and change course. It is common for inexperienced riders to look directly forward for long periods and thereby increase their risk of conflict with others.

- Match your course and speed to other sailors and riders. If space is tight, rather than running parallel to another windsurfer or kitesurfer, try slotting in behind them - this way you will be using the same sector of water as them and consequently twice as many people can use the same area.

- If you should wipe out, be aware that your board and sail lying on the water are not easily visible by larger watercraft and cannot be moved out of the way. You can minimise this risk by not attempting difficult manoeuvres or using new equipment when the water is busy.

Collision Avoidance Rules

The first thing to know about these rules is that you should never need to use them if you keep a good lookout and avoid a conflict situation arising!

- Head-on collision situation. When two craft are on opposite courses the international convention for all watercraft, is that starboard tack has priority - this means the one leading with his right shoulder has the right of way and the other craft should take avoiding action.

- Converging courses. When two craft are converging, the one to windward (upwind) shall give way. Note the use of the word 'craft' - you have an equal responsibility with any other sailing craft to take action to avoid conflict .

- Overtaking. If you are the overtaking craft, you must make sure you have been seen and take a course that will give you plenty of room to get by without any risk of collision. If you are the craft being overtaken, you must continue on your course (i.e. do not make any unexpected course changes that could increase the risk of collision).

- Jumping. When jumping ensure that the area you are using is clear of other water users for some distance downwind. Never try and jump physical obstacles such as boats, buoys, other windsurfers or swimmers.

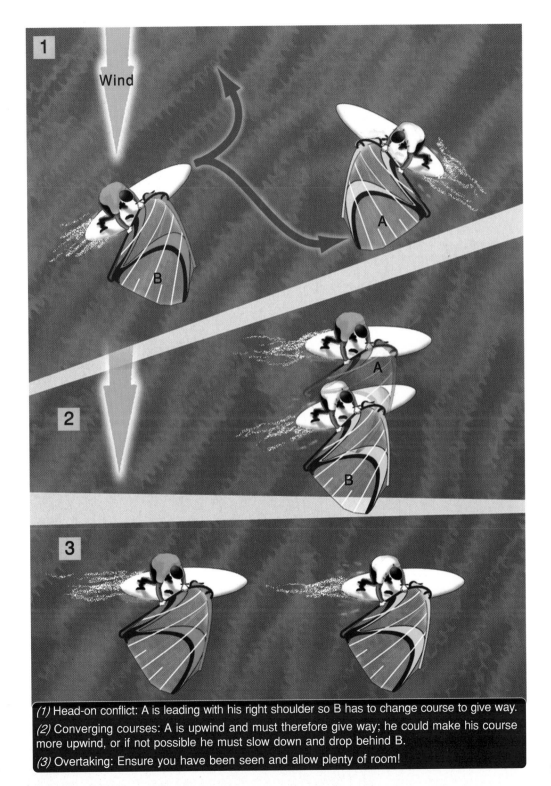

(1) Head-on conflict: A is leading with his right shoulder so B has to change course to give way.

(2) Converging courses: A is upwind and must therefore give way; he could make his course more upwind, or if not possible he must slow down and drop behind B.

(3) Overtaking: Ensure you have been seen and allow plenty of room!

- Shipping channels. If you must cross one, do so in as straight a line as possible, preferably at 90 degrees. You have no rights at all when you are in a shipping channel! Your only option is to ride defensively, keeping well away from other traffic or avoid spending much time in shipping channels. If you sail in a busy area it is well worth buying an admiralty chart that shows all the channels.

- Always ride with consideration for others. Just because you may have priority over another craft does not mean you should abuse this. Avoid impeding their paths where possible. (These are recreational safety rules of course - it is different in races, where using your right of way to your advantage is a major tactical weapon!)

Kitesurfing, sailing and many other activities are allowed in shared venues like lakes and on popular beaches. Sadly, some others - jet-skiing is the prime example - are banned from many suitable locations, and to a great extent it is because of the undisciplined behaviour of some of the riders.

Perhaps the greatest conflict occurs in inland waters when the banks are popular with fishermen; keep well away from fishing areas and land only at recognised launch areas.

Some landowners, local authorities and others will be cautious about allowing access. Asking permission, avoiding conflict with other water users and showing consideration will count heavily in our favour. We are all ambassadors of the sport!

Keep a good lookout, so you always know what is behind you

Getting Out of Trouble & Dealing With Emergencies

Like any adventure sport windsurfing carries some risks; these can be minimised by good care of the equipment, riding within your limits and particularly by exercising caution with the weather conditions. However, if you keep sailing for long enough, an unforeseen situation will eventually catch you out.

Self-help

If you cannot stay on your board: if you are overpowered, or if the wind is just too gusty, then at some point you will simply get too tired to keep trying.

Try and anticipate this situation - it is better to give up and go home too early than too late.

If you are close to shore, you can simply paddle the board; this is very tiring. But is usually slightly more efficient than trying to swim towing it (see below).

Sailing with the rig in the secure position (both hands on the mast) may help you deal with the strong wind or gusts. If you have a leg injury, it is possible to sail seated, holding the mast and the foot of the sail.

If the wind has died completely and you are drifting, you will have to start paddling.

The wind never stops suddenly, and you

Practicing self rescue

can often predict when it will start to reduce (sea breezes dying in the evening for example), so planning ahead and staying close to shore in weakening conditions will minimise the chances of being caught in this situation.

If you have lost control of the rig for some reason - perhaps the sail is damaged, or the boom or mast are broken.

Take a moment or two to assess the situation. Are you drifting inshore? Has anyone seen you? How much daylight is left? How useless is your kit? It is possible to sail with a damaged sail, or with a broken boom, especially if one side will still function. (If it's the 'wrong' side and there is a long way to go it may be worth unclamping it and turning it upside down to get the undamaged boom in the right position for sailing.

If the mast is broken, a possible option is to slide the bits out of the luff-tube and rebuild it by shoving the tapered tip of the mast into the lower section. (A break is inevitably just above the clamping reinforcement.) This makeshift mast can then be shoved back into the luff tube and will give enough rigidity to get home..

If you cannot manage this, or the wind is offshore and you do not have the time to spare, then roll up your rig and lie on the board to offer you some buoyancy as you paddle back to shore. If the nose is constantly being buried by swell, it may be practical to reverse the board and paddle tail first.

Never leave your board. It is your flotation aid.

Whilst you could simply ditch the rig, do not forget that any rescue vessel is going to have a hard time locating you and having something big and colourful to hold up or catch the sun might be critical in attracting attention.

Help From Another Windsurfer

If you are sailing with a buddy there are several ways he can help.

He could sail in to get you a replacement boom or mast, or tow you in, or he could go for help. If there is more than one other sailor, one should stay with the 'casualty'.

One windsurfer can tow another - this is surprisingly easy if the rig is all packed up. The towee simply lies on his board and grabs the mast foot of the towing board with one hand. That's it. You will not get planing, but once moving you can make very good progress.

It is also possible to hang on to the back strap of the towing board, but experience shows that this is a more difficult method, though it may be better suited to a strong swell where the boards are bouncing up and down and the mast foot is hard to grip.

To tow with a rope means you will need to find one - this may mean using your uphaul or downhaul cord(s).

Many boards are equipped with a towing eye or loop you can use, but if not, the line should be connected to the rear footstraps of each board, and off you go. Obviously in the latter case this means that the towed board is going backwards, but it works surprisingly well, and as the maximum buoyancy is located at the back of most modern boards, the problems of burying the nose of the towed board in waves is largely avoided. Either tow technique can be adapted for being towed by almost any craft, such as a jet ski, dinghy or canoe.

If you are downwind of your beach, paddling or being towed may make upwind progress difficult. You may have to reconsider where you land. It is better to get to shore in the wrong place and walk, or have your buddy go for help, than be left drifting at sea where you will be very hard to locate again.

Help From Other Vessels

If you need help, the international signal for distress is to wave both arms symmetrically from the water line to above your head. If you are OK (i.e. do not need help), the signal is to place one hand or both hands on your head.

Be careful to keep your rig out of the way if calling a vessel to your aid, as sails and propellers do not mix well. If possible, signal or shout to them to approach you from upwind.

It is important that you always know where you are. If you are sailing in an unfamiliar area do not venture too far - it is easy to lose sight of landmarks if you are low in the sea with a swell.

· Always sail within your abilities and with others, and if you do sail out at sea you may consider investing in some rocket flares. They are no bigger than a pack of cigarettes and can be stowed in a

Distress signal ~ I need help

pocket of your harness.

If you are rescued by a helicopter, the down-draught from the rotors will push your board away from the winch man or flip it over. In this situation you may have to swim away from the board to be rescued.

If it all goes pear-shaped and you do abandon your sail, or even your board, when you are picked up, it is very important (and a legal requirement the UK) that you inform the coastguard of what has happened.

In North-East England in January 2002, a kitesurfer lost his kite, which was later spotted drifting by a fisherman. The ensuing air-sea rescue effort involved a lifeboat and two helicopters and cost over £38,000. The rider had just

Hitching a ride back in

abandoned his kit and gone home. This kind of thing does not endear us to the rescue services.

Medical Emergencies

Most of the above assumes that you are the casualty and that you are in reasonable shape.

The biggest hazards to windsurfers are the potential for getting a lung full of water and drowning. And suffering from either hypothermia or dehydration.

Drowning

If a fellow sailor gets stunned or manages to get water in his lungs in some way, the first priority is to clear the airway. This usually means getting his face out of the water, but it can also mean tilting his chin back if he has lost consciousness, as his tongue could block his airway. The second priority is to call for help, if possible, or to send someone else to do so.

If he is not breathing, the third priority is to get some air into his system (don't bother trying to get the water out first). This is best done with mouth-to-mouth resuscitation - obviously very difficult in a swell with someone draped halfway across a sinky little board. But if the heart is still beating, one or two breaths might just jump-start the breathing reflex.

CPR (heart massage) is not practical in these circumstances, and research shows that a stopped heart has to be defibrillated within no more than about 12 minutes to have any chance at all of restarting.

Hypothermia

Hypothermia is a very real danger when sailing in colder water; good equipment is vital and knowing your own limits is the key to sailing safely.

Hypothermia is a drop in the body's core temperature, and an effective way to achieve it is to combine wet skin with wind, resulting in a very high windchill factor.

Being in cold water for prolonged periods is much more likely to kill you by hypothermia than by drowning.

Hypothermia comes on gradually, so learn to recognise the warning signs of shivering, pale skin, apathy, irrational

behaviour, disorientation and sometimes belligerence.

The symptoms may not manifest themselves until the sailor is on the shore - stripping off in a windy car park could be the final straw..

Treatment is to get warm and dry, and give warm drinks and high-energy food like chocolate.

Do not allow the casualty any alcohol. Do not place the casualty close to a direct heart source.

If the casualty lies down or loses consciousness ensure that he is insulated from the ground.

Anyone who show signs of hypothermia should not be left alone, and medical treatment should be sought.

So, to recap - anyone seen shivering and looking pale, or who seems belligerent, irrational or apathetic after windsurfing should not be bought a drink. (That should save a few quid!)

Sunburn, Dehydration and Heat Exhaustion

Sunburn

When on the water, a high proportion of the sun's radiation is reflected upward from the surface, so the sailor is receiving a much higher dose of UV than if he were just lying on the beach.

Because the wind is cooling you by evaporating sweat and spray from your skin (the windchill factor as mentioned above) the heat of sun is not as apparent, and the result is that it is much easier to get burned.

This is unpleasant, and peeling feet and faces are not very attractive. An overdose of sun can make you feel ill and spoil your sailing, (and even your holiday) and sunburn is a major factor in the increasing incidence of skin cancer.

Too much sun is bad news. The only way to combat this is to cover up by wearing a rash vest and a hat - unless you are very confident, this will need a cord under your chin!

Sunglasses are also useful, but again they need a cord or croakie so you do not lose them.

Any skin left exposed should be liberally slathered with high factor waterproof sun cream (with the notable exception of the soles of the feet!).

If you have been burned and have red skin, regular sun cream will not prevent more damage the next day - the only option is to cover up or use total sun block.

Note: lips are notoriously prone to wind and sunburn, and the protection soon wears off, so use a separate chap-stick and re-apply often.

Dehydration

It may seem a bit strange to be concerned by dehydration when doing a watersport, but however wet you are, you can still lack water on the inside!

As a windsurfer may be very active, out for long periods sweating profusely and probably also wearing a wetsuit with no handy pockets for a water bottle, this is not uncommon.

Thirst, headaches and possibly dizziness are the early symptoms. But by the time you feel dry-mouthed you are already suffering from serious dehydration.

You should drink before you are thirsty. For most sailors this means topping up on water (not sugary drinks, tea and coffee or beer!) before you venture out for a session.

Note: a possible cause of raised body temperature is the use of some recreational drugs, particularly Ecstasy, which can cause profuse sweating and accelerate the onset of serious dehydration.

Take a bottle of water to the beach with you and keep topping up whenever you come ashore. If you are fresh off the aeroplane and sailing in a hotter climate than usual, this is doubly important.

Heat exhaustion

Heat exhaustion is the next stage if dehydration or sunburn is not treated, or if the casualty is already suffering from fluid loss through recent sickness or diarrhoea.

The symptoms are like dehydration but with cramps, weakness, dizziness and confusion, a rapid pulse and 'panting' respiration.

The treatment is to get the casualty cooled down (by lying in the water) giving water to drink and, if possible, some weak salt solution. Recovery can seem quick, but it takes some time to recover fully and it is advisable to seek medical attention.

In severe cases or if left untreated this can develop into heat stroke, which is very dangerous and can lead to unconsciousness. This is recognisable by a 'bounding' pulse and red flushed skin. Sweating stops. Heat stroke requires hospitalisation.

14 Using a Harness

You can sail a windsurfer without a harness, so why use one?

A harness has three primary functions:

The first is very simple - it relieves the load on your arms and shoulders, and allows you to sail for longer, and in stronger winds, without getting tired.

The second function is that by hooking in your harness you are locked into a position where your hips and waist are held forwards, and to balance the pull of the rig you must lean back with your shoulders and position your body and the rig differently.

This is the basis of the correct stance you need to sail well.

Thirdly, the harness also allows you to transmit the power of the sail slightly differently, both directly though your legs and down through the mast foot. This balance of force is very helpful in controlling the attitude and direction of your board.

Photo: Bicsport

Harness Types

The standard harness type for many years was the seat or slalom harness: this gives a low connection point and allows a very committed reclining position. It is still a good choice, particularly for holding down well powered rigs. Its advan-

Seat harness

Waist harness

tage is that it can be teamed with a buoyancy aid. However, some wave sailors soon found that it was difficult to hook in and out as quickly as they wished and to address this problem, tried sailing with chest harnesses, very similar to those used by dinghy sailors for trapeze work. These are now rarely seen, as the advent of the waist harness has proved a good solution for most sailors. The waist harness is good for beginners, too, as it is quick to put on and is easy to hook in and out with. The limited buoyancy is helpfully located above the sailor's centre of gravity.

A downside is that a separate buoyancy aid cannot be worn with a waist harness.

Many modern seat harnesses now incorporate a support panel for the lower back as well, effectively making them similar to a waist harness in feel.

Preparation

A harness must fit snugly, and the hook should be tight to the harness and located centrally. If using a school harness this may mean spending a few minutes trying different sizes and adjusting the straps holding the bar. A seat harness will need the leg straps adjusting as well, and any loose straps should be tucked away so that they do not foul the hook.

You may see some harnesses with a pulley wheel in place of a hook: these work very well to help minimise wear on your harness lines, though they are primarily designed for kitesurfing.

The Lines

Your harness lines are usually cords encased in a protective plastic sheath that helps stiffen and hold them in position. The lines will have some adjustment mechanism so that you can alter the position on the boom and the length. It they are in the wrong position or are the wrong length, you will not be able to get much benefit from using a harness. The first task, therefore, is to check that the lines are correctly positioned and adjusted before leaving the beach.

The best way to position the lines is to hold up the sail in a clean wind and feel for the balance point. If you can find this with one hand the outside edges of your fist (or a bit wider) are a good starting point for the lines' attachments.

For light wind sailing, set the lines equidistant from the balance point, and for fast planing set them slightly rearward of this position, to allow for the centre of effort moving rearwards and the appar-

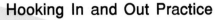

ent wind phenomenon which dictates sheeting in a little more than normal.

Length is a matter of personal preference, and depends on the height you have set the boom and the type of harness. However, because the rig will be raked back when planing, setting the lines long enough to hook in whilst standing completely upright next to the mast means they are likely to be too long. Most sailors start by using lines a little too long for optimum performance, but gradually shorten them and move them back as they improve and seek higher speeds. Slack lines mean that you will keep unhooking by mistake, which can be disconcerting.

A good rule of thumb to start with is to set the lines approximately the same length as your elbow to wrist (watch strap position) see photo opposite.

The lines should be set with just enough space to grip the boom with your fist between them. If they are set too wide they can deaden the feedback and feel from the sail. Some freestyle sailors may set them almost touching for maximum manoeuvrability.

Hooking In and Out Practice

Have a try on the beach or a simulator before you venture out. Because the hook is fairly high, you need to tilt your hips and/or rise onto your toes for a moment to locate the hook. This feels quite disconcerting initially, as you can now no longer get away from the rig! In order to de-power and sheet out the technique is now slightly different - you must now twist your hips forward and ease away with the back hand. This reduces the power without allowing the rig to fall away from your body. Sheeting in, of course, is achieved with the opposite movement combined with leaning out.

If you find you are being pulled forward when overpowering and trying to sheet out, the reaction is to try and unhook. However, once twisted forward with the sail pulling you, any motion toward the sail is impossible without being pulled over. Dealing with excess power when hooked in is a question of twisting forward and squatting down to prevent being pulled forward. This will enable you to pull the rig towards you and stay in control.

If you do follow the rig, you will find that you cannot find the slack to unhook until you are lying almost on top of the sail in the water. Once you are toppling, the best policy is to remain braced with both hands on the boom until the rig is in the water. If you are quick you can unhook and scramble back onto the board without getting wet. If you do fall right in on the sail, let go with one hand and use it to unhook manually.

Committing

Most sailors get hooked in and then take most of the weight with their arms as before! Try and make a conscious effort to let your arms relax and the harness do the work. A good tip is to uncurl your fingers and pretend you are playing a piano on the boom!

Before you know it you will be picking your nose with the best of them! You may

find that in order to load the mast foot sufficiently you will have to shorten the harness lines somewhat as you gain experience and are planing faster and more often.

Your automatic reaction to a gust should be to lean out and keep your shoulders 'open'. Try and avoid the temptation to turn toward the sail or stand upright.

Catapulting

Some sailors are reluctant to hook in because they are worried about getting catapulted into the sail.

Don't worry: this a myth - it cannot happen!

Even if it were possible, it would not be very common, and the few moments of moderate pain and bruising would be worth it for the huge benefits offered by a harness all the rest of the time!

If you are being pulled hard off the board, try to hang on to the boom with both hands - it is not always possible but it minimises the chances of damage to yourself and to your kit. In overpowered situations adopt the "drop and dig" stance, drop your hips and bend the knees, bringing your shoulders below the boom height.

Using a harness is quite traumatic for the first few attempts, but after gaining some experience with one, you may one day find yourself sailing without one and feel quite naked!

Let the harness do the work *(Photo: Bicsport)*

The Points of Sailing, Vectors & Apparent Wind

The Points of Sailing

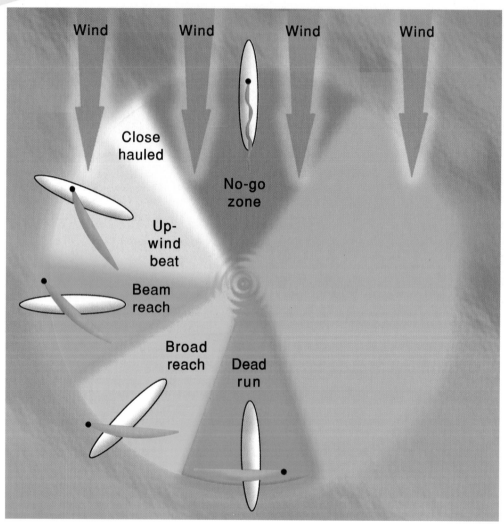

The diagram represents a plan view of all the possible directions available, with you at the centre. The exact angles will vary depending on the board being used and other factors. The wind, of course, is trying to push you straight downwind, but because you can vector this force (discussed below), you can actually sail on any course shown in the shaded area.

No-go zone

If you try and turn too far upwind, the sail will simply stop generating power and you will slow down and will have to bear away (i.e. turn to a slightly less upwind course), to start moving again. The no-go zone is therefore an effective brake; turn upwind and you will soon stop.

Sailing up-wind

You can make progress upwind by tacking. The word 'tacking' is used in sailing to describe two things: the action of turning your craft by using its momentum to force the nose of the craft through the upwind no-go sector in order to change direction, or sailing on a predominantly upwind course.

To ride to a point windward (upwind) of you, it is necessary to sail an upwind course and then make a neat efficient tack and do the same the other way, in the zigzag pattern shown.

Certain board designs with long rails and daggerboards are better at upwind courses. Some sails are also more effective than others, and the wind strength also affects the possible course, so the exact angle you can achieve can vary considerably.

However in broad terms a long board in a good breeze with a race sail is far more efficient than a shorter board in a lighter wind.

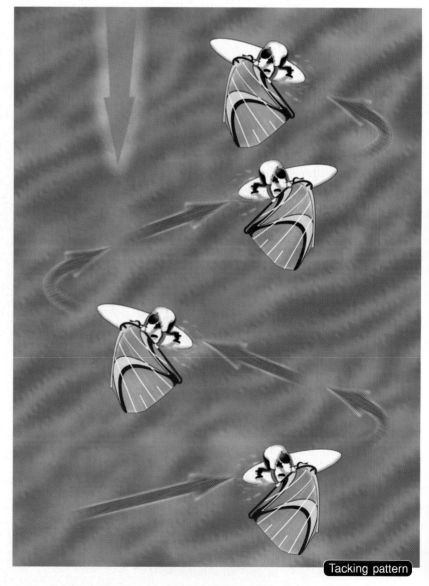

Tacking pattern

Beam reach

This simply means sailing a course at roughly cross wind. A perfect beam reach is 90 degrees to the wind, but the term is used for any more-or-less cross-wind beat.

Because holding a beam reach track or a slightly upwind track means you are burning up a lot of your available energy on combating the lateral drag, this course is slower than a broad reach in the same wind conditions.

Broad reach

This is the fastest point of sailing - almost all the sail's power is driving in the desired direction, and the lack of lateral movement minimises

Broad reach; off the plane. Note the 'open' rig position.
(Photo: J Carter, Starboard)

drag. In lighter winds, a good way to get planing is to work your way upwind for a few tacks, then turn onto a broad reach for a high-speed blast or two back to your start point. Once planing well, your drag is reduced, and you can often ease the board smoothly back round on to a beam reach without coming off the plane.

Because of the apparent wind (see below), the rig is often close hauled again when sailing fast

Close hauled for upwind progress

The dead run

If you try and head dead downwind, the sail loses much of the power generated by the action of the airfoil. Added to this, the only way to control the remaining power of the sail is to step right back, sinking the tail of the board. Speed is lost and the board soon comes off the plane and wallows. The only way to prevent this is by turning slightly; the whole system powers up again and you are off on a broad reach.

It is possible to sink the tail of the board and travel directly downwind - this is a useful exercise when practising your flare gybes, but you can progress in the desired direction much more efficiently with a few beats on a broad reach.

Dead run downwind. Stepping back to control the power of the rig.
(Photo: J Carter, Starboard)

Vectors

When a force acting in one direction, such as the wind, is deflected or harnessed to generate a force in a different direction, it is known as vectoring. The sail itself vectors the wind using its airfoil to generate a forward force, and the board vectors the force transmitted through the rider's feet to travel cross-wind or upwind.

A nice analogy for this is a bicycle. Ride the bike over a cliff, and the force (gravity in this case) will act directly on you!

Roll down a slope, and the same force pulling the same way now provides a forward motion - the hill has vectored the force. Steer at an angle across the slope, and it can be vectored even more, until eventually you will be going at close to 90 degrees to the original force and it will stop.

Unfortunately, no-one has managed the trick of vectoring gravity so far that you can roll a bike uphill, but that is exactly what windsurfing does with our primary force: the wind. (Damn clever, eh?)

Apparent Wind

When you are riding at some speed, you will start to notice that the fastest course is not a constant direction but is curving downwind. To hold your course and speed, you need to sheet in further and load the rear foot slightly more.

What you are experiencing is the phenomenon we call apparent wind.

Wind is the name we give to moving air masses, but of course it feels the same and behaves the same way if it is you that is actually doing the moving.

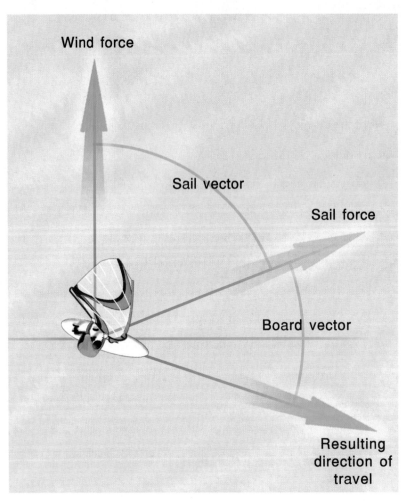

Wind force

Sail vector

Sail force

Board vector

Resulting direction of travel

Imagine you are in a speed boat doing, say, 20 knots (roughly 22mph) on a still day.

The 'wind' will be 20 knots in your face - if you launched a kite it would fly behind you.

On the same boat, travelling at the same speed but at 90 degrees to a 'real' 20-knot wind, the apparent wind direction would be from midway between the true wind and the speed-through-the-air of the boat, and the kite now would fly at an angle behind you.

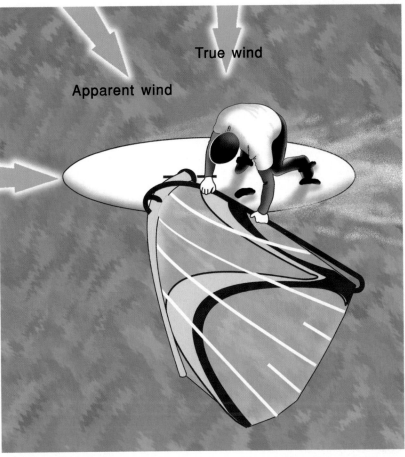

True wind

Apparent wind

This is exactly the situation with windsurfing at speed - as your board moves faster, so the apparent wind is coming from more ahead of you. To control this you need to sheet in more as you speed up.

As your board speed increases and the apparent wind phenomena occurs, you are not only changing the wind's direction, but you are also effectively increasing the windspeed, so the sail generates more power. This is why during the first part of a planing beat with steady wind,

you should expect to be able to gradually accelerate.

Eventually, the drag will balance the forward motion and the apparent wind will force you to change course downwind if you want to go faster.

This point of maximum speed is good time to try a carve gybe!

Planing

Move a windsurf board fast enough, and it will start to generate lift and rise out of the water. As it does so, the board is no longer pushing through the water and displacing the water to the sides, but is skimming over the surface.

The key to planing is to be moving fast, and for that you need to have plenty of power, so a good wind is necessary to provide that speed.

If there is a very strong wind then almost all you need to do is hang-on! However, most sailors progress to planing in moderate winds to start with; this means that the skills of helping the board and sail act together as an efficient system must be mastered in order to succeed.

Like all new skills, the first step is to visualise how it is going to work and imagine skimming effortlessly over the waves. If your mind is ready, your body will often follow! If you are frightened of going fast, or falling off, or do not expect to succeed, the task becomes much more difficult.

The theory of planing is covered in Chapter 11. If you understand how it works, it is easier to know what actions are required to remedy any problems.

Start by selecting a big enough sail to give you sufficient power, and a suitable board.

Once moving well on a beam reach, lean the rig to push the nose onto a broad reach (more downwind) course. Ensure that your dagger board is retracted.

Photo: Bicsport

As the power of the sail increases, you will be stepping back to compensate, but as you speed up you also want to flatten the board, in order to push the nose over the stagnation point and reduce drag from the sinking tail.

To do this, you must get weight back on to the front of the board. As your most forward point of contact is the mast, you must shift some weight from your feet to the mast foot. If you are not yet using a harness, you need to 'hang' on your front arm to achieve this, but a more comfortable method is to transmit as much weight as you can through your harness. Once hooked in, start leaning forwards, down and out, to load the boom through the harness lines, as if you are trying to look around the front of the mast foot.

This position feels a little weird initially, but it is effective in loading the board correctly.

Think back to your theory - speed is a result of squeezing the board between the power of the sail and the resistance of the fin. You can aid this process by driving against the fin and increasing the squeeze. You may see some sailors pumping furiously in marginal conditions to try and get planing primarily by leg power!

In contrast to this, the next tip is that once things are getting going, keep everything still! Many new sailors move back and forth on the board, or sheet in and out with the sail. By all means feel for the best point, but make all your movements smooth and progressive. If there is another experienced sailor in front of you, try and emulate his course, and his sail and body position.

This may not work the first time, but if you keep trying it is inevitable that you will soon find you are blasting with the best of them.

Using a harness holds your hips forwards and allows you to keep your body straight - this is less tiring and again helps transmit the power effectively. When starting to sail fast, the tendency is to load

This young sailor is transmitting the power through his front leg, but is putting no pressure on the mast foot, and as a result the board is nose high and cannot plane. He must either lean out and forward, loading his front arm or, preferably, hook in and load the harness and therefore the mast foot.

the back of the board as you oppose the sail trying to pull you forward, but this can make the board nose-high and makes it much harder to start planing (which needs a flat board). Using a harness helps you to put pressure through the foot of the mast, keeping the board flat and making planing much easier.

It also cuts the arms and waist out of

the 'power train' and allows more direct transmission of the sail's force to the board.

By flexing at the waist, elbows, or knees, the body acts as a shock absorber and can dissipate a good portion of the power. A good tip for maximum speed is to tense all your muscles and stiffen your joints: 'locking up' like this can add a surprising edge of extra speed!.

Once established in the plane you can sheet in a little more and curve your course back towards a beam reach (crosswind) without losing speed.

Once the board is planing comfortably, the control becomes much more subtle, with foot pressure becoming the main mechanism for steering, and the rig remaining fairly still.

As you speed up, the leaning forward 'peering around the mast' position is altered to reflect the stagnation point of the water under the board moving back. As you move your weight back to balance the force of the rig and keep the whole thing trimmed, you will find that the rig will need to be raked back with you.

At full blast on a broad reach you will have your feet well back, and your body leaning out and back with the sail foot almost touching the deck.

Related information on planing can be found in Chapter 10: How the Board Works and in Chapter 15: The Points of Sailing, Vectors and the Apparent Wind.

The keys to successful planing:

- **Sufficient power** (the right sail and enough wind).
- **Drag reduction** (a broad reach, daggerboard up, the right board).
- **Stance** (hooked in, shoulders open, looking ahead, mast-foot pressure).
- **Trim** (sheeted in the right amount).
- **Space** (a long enough reach to get going).
- **Confidence**

Photo: Bicsport

Using the Footstraps

All new boards are supplied with footstraps. For the early exercises they are more of a nuisance than a help, but as the board begins to plane they become an important part of the system.

Footstraps are usually made of a combination of webbing, neoprene and velcro; their purpose is to give a secure anchor position for your feet. Most obviously they prevent your feet sliding around or bouncing out of position when riding fast over choppy water. And reduce your chances of being pulled forward off the board. But although these are important functions, they are not always the primary purpose of using the straps initially.

By securing your feet in the correct position on the board, the straps force you to adopt a good stance and load the board correctly.

Of course, once your feet are slotted in, you can no longer move them around - although this takes some getting used to, it will pay dividends in improving your technique.

By 'locking' you to the board and making the system more rigid, the straps also help you with applying appropriate pressure, both for foot steering, and for effectively transmitting the power of the sail through the board.

The first time you try using the straps you will find it feels distinctly weird and insecure, but don't worry - with a bit of practice, using them will become second nature.

Fitting

You may need to locate and fit the straps yourself. The manufacturer will have provided a choice of screw location holes

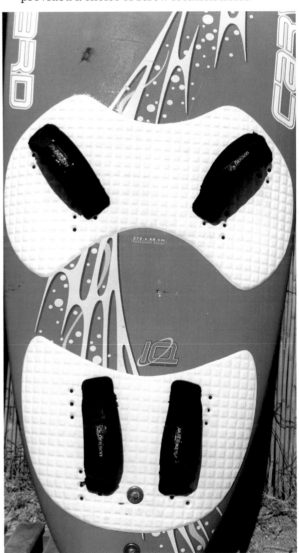

on most boards; to begin with, your best option is to choose the most forward positions for the straps. This makes them easiest to get in and out of, and is probably the closest to your natural foot position at this stage.

There are (generally) two front straps and two rear ones. On many modern wider boards the rear straps are situated well apart, close to the rear rail. Initially, choose the positions closest to the centre line of the board. (You may well find the front screw holes are slightly inboard in any case.) This advice does vary, depending on the design of board.

A few boards offer a strap position that is so far forward you can stand and sail the board in very light winds with your feet in the straps. This is of little use, other than to help get used to the idea, and they will need to be moved back to be in the planing foot position.

Too loose

Too tight

Adjustment

The straps should be adjusted so that they are snug over the widest part of your foot. Adjustment is either by a buckle of some kind, or by velcro straps. If using velcro make sure the 'hooks' are completely covered by the fabric sleeves, as it is very abrasive and can easily damage the neoprene material of your boots.

Just right!

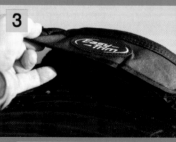

Adjusting the footstraps.

If the straps are too tight they will be very hard to locate and your feet will either slip out because they are not properly located, or even worse, the foot will be jammed in hard and be difficult to remove.

Very loose straps may also mean your feet slipping out, or in an extreme situation that even the whole foot can pass through, trapping your ankle. Do not forget that you may need to adjust your straps if you are swapping from a climate where thick boots are needed to one where you may sail in bare feet!

If using a hired or borrowed board, it is well worth spending a few minutes on the beach checking the straps before venturing out.

Ideally, your foot should rest comfortably in the strap, but you should not be able to push your foot in so far that the strap touches the vertical part of your ankle.

Using the Straps

When your are planing comfortably, balance your weight evenly between the rear foot and your harness until you find that there is little load on the front foot.

This is the moment to move it and slip it into the front strap. When you have done this a few times you will find that locating the front strap is quick and easy. Many sailors struggle with the straps by trying to go for both straps very quickly. Take your time and get used to sailing with only one foot in for a while.

A common worry is falling off with the feet in the straps - in fact the more secure footing afforded by the straps helps you to resist that first critical step, and to a great extent can prevent you being pulled over the front.

In any case, if they are well adjusted, the straps will normally release your feet easily as you automatically 'kick out' and your foot will rotate easily from the strap as you fall.

It is worth finding this out for yourself and developing confidence with one strap before progressing on to both.

When you are comfortable in the front strap and your back foot is located just in front or on top of the rear straps, it is time to slot in the back foot. A good way to do this is to pivot the foot on your heel and then slide it into the strap without ever losing contact with the deck of the board. A common problem is to overload the back foot and to cause the board to start heading up into wind. To counter this, you must apply more mast foot pressure through the harness by leaning further forward and out.

Pivoting the back foot into the rear strap.

This leaning forward, committed to the harness stance is the classic 'go faster' position and will help keep your board flat and fast.

As you use the straps in stronger winds (or with bigger sails) you will discover that the board is planing further back on the undersurface and you need to lean further back yourself, raking the sail back with you. Before long you will feel the urge to step a bit further back to keep the whole thing in equilibrium. This is when the screwdriver comes out again and the straps need shifting back and out a bit further.

Shorter, narrower boards will need the rear straps very close together, and in many of the smallest boards, the rear strap is just a single item located over the centre line of the board, with the rails being controlled by heel and toe pressure.

If you are jumping, the straps are obviously critical to keep you attached to the board. However, if you lose one strap it is advisable to kick off the other as well, as landing with one foot connected can significantly increase the risk of picking up an injury.

Some sailors get into the straps early but still use their knees as shock absorbers to iron out the bumps and keep the power

Photo: Bicsport

controlled. This works to some extent, but to really capitalise on the available power try locking your arms, back and legs into a rigid triangle and driving all the power directly though the feet and straps to push the board forward. Not only does this increase your speed - it also makes the whole system feel more secure.

After sailing in the straps for a while, getting back on a planing board without them feels distinctly weird and insecure!

Love is... one footstrap each! *(Photo: Bicsport)*

18 Beach Starting

Beach staring is a very useful skill, you stay drier than if you wade out with your board and then up-haul, and in any kind of swell or waves it is much easier.

When you progress to lower volume boards it is the only practical way to start.

In order to beach start you must first position the board correctly. And there must be at least some breeze to help you.

Place the board in the water pointing slightly downwind, with sufficient depth to ensure the fin does not ground. At this stage the dagger board will be retracted.

Stand on the upwind side of the board with your front hand on the mast, and rear hand on the boom.

You can now steer the board by applying pressure through the mast foot. Push the mast downward and forward, and the board will bear away downwind; lift and pull the mast, and the board will pivot on the fin and head back up into the wind.

This is harder to master if there are waves breaking around you, but a judicious nudge of the knee can help hold the board where you want it. If the wind is directly offshore, the board should be pointed slightly across the wind, and will be pushed around by the waves. If the wind is directly onshore you will need to start from deeper water. Both these problems can be overcome with good technique, but it is harder, so if in doubt - wait for a better day.

It is worth spending some time mastering this steering by mast foot pressure, as it will be a very useful tool in your box of tricks!

Once the board is in position, lift the rig slightly so that you can feel the wind pulling you. If the rig is heavy or trying to flip, your position must be wrong - try pushing the nose away a little further. Orientate the sail so that if it were vertical you would be sailing on a broad reach.

Do not try and force the sail upward by brute force. From almost any position it can be persuaded to adopt the correct one with the correct technique. Stand upwind of the rig and, holding the mast with one hand, feel for the point at which it is trying to fly upward. This is your start point.

Once balanced, place your back foot onto the centre line of the board. Exactly where will depend on the strength of the breeze.

Push the rig up and step up with your front leg as the sail helps you. Imagine there is a friend pulling the rig from the other side and you are springing up onto a step. Do not pull the rig towards you, but follow it up.

If there is plenty of wind, the rig may try to pull you right over the board! In this case, stay low and step on a little further back, or orientate the board a few more degrees into wind.

With practice you will soon find that you can beach start from slightly deeper water. This is often necessary with the long fins fitted to many boards, if the water depth drops off quickly or if the wind is onshore.

Initially, the back foot will only be hooked

Deep water beach sta

onto the board by the heel, and you may be poised on tiptoe on your remaining foot, but the principle is the same. Throwing the rig forward and up keeping your arms extended helps the boost up onto the board, a common fault is pulling the rig down as you step up.

With practice, you will find that as long as the rig is flying and there is a reason-able breeze, you can dispense with the foot on the bottom altogether and lie back in the water to lift the back heel on. (This is much easier with a buoyancy aid)

This is very useful technique to master, not only for a neat beach start, but be-cause it is also the basis of the waterstart, which will save you from (almost) all that uphauling in the future.

Water Starting

When windsurfers began to sail the waves on a regular basis and boards gradually shrank to meet the requirements of this environment, the technique of water-starting - which until then had been a 'trick' practised by a few freestyle sailors - became a vital tool.

Small sails and boards, strong winds combined with seas too rough for standing up on the board, and pulling a sail from the water, guaranteed that this technique was soon adopted by any serious sailor. Anyone who has experienced the satisfaction of performing an elegant water-start is not about to go back to up-hauling if they can avoid it.

Once mastered, the water-start enables the sailor to use much smaller and more manoeuvrable boards and sails (and fall off!) in wavy conditions that would be hazardous if they had to rely on up-hauling alone.

Technique: the technique is very similar to the beach start - the only problem is that after a speedy wipe-out the sail is quite likely to be on the wrong (leeward) side of the board and immersed in the water. The first task, then, is to get the rig into position.

Rig Recovery

If the rig is on the downwind side, you need to move it to the back, or slightly upwind side, of the board. At the same time, you must be working to end up with the mast at 90 degrees to the wind. This is achieved by swimming the rig towards the rear of the board and pushing the board under the boom. Which route you choose obviously depends on which is the shortest way to end up with the board

pointing on a broad reach with the mast across the wind.

How easy it is to get the boom over the tail depends on the height of your boom and the length of your board. If the boom will sit on the tail of the board this is very helpful for getting it clear of the water. If not, it is easier to pull it around to the upwind side.

Assuming that the boom does sit on the tail (or on your forearm, which is on the tail), the wind can already get under the sail in this position, and may try to lift it. The battens may need to be popped through so that the airfoil section is operating the right way up. (Some sails with cams will need a good thump to achieve this.)

Getting air under the sail is known as 'flying the rig', and caution must be taken in stronger winds, or the boom can be whipped out of your hands and splash down back where it came from on the far side of the board!

You may need to 'flip' the rig if it is clew upwind, to get it to the luff (mast) upwind position.

However, the most common situation during early attempts at water starting is that the sailor gets the rig into the right position but has trouble getting the rig to fly. The more the mast is lifted, the more the clew sinks.

The key point is to get rid of any water on the top of the sail before trying to fly it.

This can be done by heaving it forward into wind and over your head in one powerful motion - this both drains the water from the top and gets the air flowing underneath the sail. This technique is very physical, and can be very tiring if you need to repeat it. In a good breeze (which is when it works best), it may be hard to control with only one hand, when it does work. With practice, you can combine the tasks of lifting the rig over the tail and flying it in one smooth motion. Expert sailors may wipe out and then seem to resurrect themselves with an

Resting the boom on an arm

the area "shown" to the wind.

A good kick with the leg in the water can help with boosting you up onto the board.

If the wind is light this demands a good technique - remember, the more sail area you can 'show' the wind, the more power is available. So point the board more downwind and throw the rig as high as possible. Some sailors will drop one hand down the mast, below the boom,

Putting both feet on the board too early is much less effective unless the wind is very strong

almost instant water start in this way. (Very handy if you are between waves!)

An easier alternative is to simply 'bounce' the mast up and down gently. This action pumps air under the sail, and each pump drains a little more water from the top, floating the clew. The rig starts to fly at a very low angle, which you can then increase in a controlled manner with both hands already on the boom.

Once the rig is flying, the rest is easy: using mast foot pressure in exactly the same way as a beach start, manoeuvre the board to point onto the course you want. Hooking the board with your rear heel and 'pulling ' it towards you is also helpful. Place your rear heel onto the board, and then allow the sail to lift, In lighter winds, "throwing " it forward with a straight front arm will increase

and grasp the foot of the sail instead of the boom with the back hand, allowing the rig to rotate fully upright or beyond as they are pulled up.

In strong winds the danger is in being pulled right over the front of the board, so the key is to keep the rig and body low during the whole manoeuvre.

A good way to practice the water start is to do it backwards.. Try dropping your front leg into the water and maintaining control as you sail; it is helpful to squat fairly low to do this, and this also mimics the water start position.

From here is a small step to allow yourself to subside gently backwards into the water, but keep the rig flying, and try and recover from there.

Foot dragging is good practice and in a

good wind you can step of the board completely for a body drag. (See picture overleaf and right at the front of the book!)

In stronger winds, stay low as you mount the board. The force of the sail on a stationary board will be very powerful as it tries to accelerate, and as you step up the burst of power can flip you straight back out of the front door again. If the board tries to pivot back up into wind as your rear foot loads the tail, combat this with additional mast foot pressure.

Up and away: keeping the body low

The key to strong winds is keeping the mast low - if it gets too high and the clew dips into the water the rig will pivot on the clew and be flipped out of your hands.

The key (as always) is to practice, and an hour or two spent in chest-deep water getting the technique right will pay dividends when you are in deeper water.

Let the wind do the hard work so you don't have to. If you are struggling to lift the mast or throw it forward, go back a step and practice flying the rig in shallower water.

Eventually, if your sailing is always in planing conditions, it is practical to waterstart every time. However, be cautious about throwing away your uphaul cord.

If you are ever stuck with the wind dropping fast, you may just need it again one day.

Uphauling a low-volume board (though challenging) can be done with good technique.

Photo: Gun

Understanding the Weather

Forecasts

Like almost all outdoor activities, we first need to decide what the weather is going to be like so that we can choose our venue or choose to stay at home.

Step one is simply looking out of the window, but the problem here is that you can only see what is it like now. What you need is to know how the weather will develop during the next few hours, and for that you need a forecast.

TV is very good on general weather, If it will be sunny or if it will be windy for example. From this you can gain a good idea of whether conditions are worth checking out further, the better TV forecasts feature a synoptic chart with isobars (lines joining points of equal pressure) and frontal systems.

This type of chart is also available from the met office as a fax, or on the internet.

The simple rule when checking out a synoptic chart is that the closer together the isobars, the stronger the wind will be. The wind strength and direction will be shown at various points on a chart but, inevitably, not just where you want! To know the direction at a given spot, you do need to be able to 'read' the chart yourself.

Useful forecasts can also be gained from the radio; the best of these in the UK is undoubtedly the Radio 4 shipping forecast (broadcast daily at 17.50). This gives actual readings from coastal stations and sea areas.

Of course you do need to know where the sea areas are. (See map overleaf)

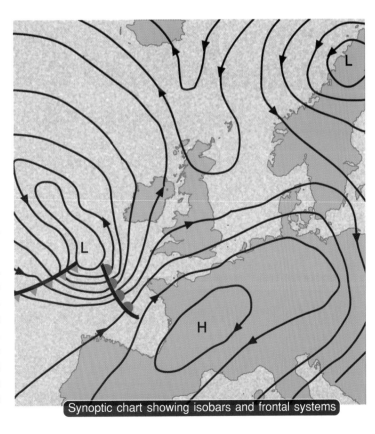

Synoptic chart showing isobars and frontal systems

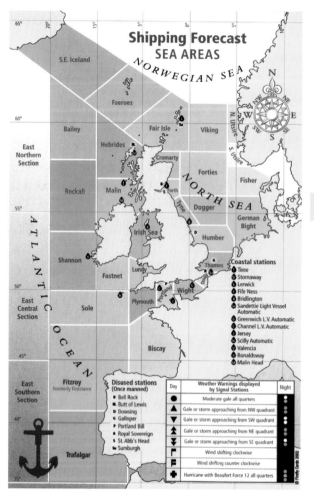

Shipping Forecast
SEA AREAS

conditions now and the trend over the last hour or two. The 'wendy windblows ' coastal stations are especially useful as they are located at favourite windsurfing and kitesurfing spots and they also give tide states.

Details can be found at www.wendy-windblows .com

Basic Meteorology

The weather is a huge and complex subject, but a grasp of the basic mechanics of a weather system will help you plan your venue more accurately and give you a good idea of what to expect next. Here is the quick guide to the main features:

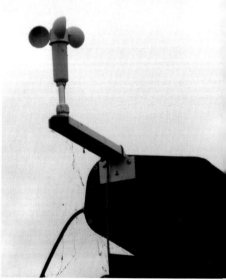

Weather station measuring head

Finally, there are a number of telephone forecasts that are available; these vary considerably between 'it will be a nice day' to good accurate wind and weather data. In the UK almost all get their information from the met office and you can get a list of what forecasts are available. Forecast details are listed in the 'information' section.

Some sailing, windsurfing and other sports clubs now have their own automated weather stations that you can access by phone. These give you the exact

Depressions and Fronts

Depressions are areas of relatively low atmospheric pressure. Air can rise easily in these regions and as a result depressions are frequently associated with cloud and rain. Depressions often form where air masses of different temperatures meet. The division between these air masses is known as a front. Because the air masses on either side of the front have different characteristics, these fronts become irregular and develop 'waves' along their length. The actual process is largely triggered by the high altitude jetstream winds.

A wave on the front is the first sign of a depression being created.

As the depression develops, the pressure drops, and the winds increase. The air masses are now arranged in sectors, and are typically divided by a warm front followed by a cold front (shown on the chart on page 139).

As the depression gradually fills and weakens over the course of a few days, the cold front gradually overtakes the warm front and the result is an occluded front. Occlusions can be just like having one front turning into the next, giving miserable conditions for many hours, but quite often they are fairly weak and are marked by nothing more than a thickening band of cloud for an hour or two, or a few spots of rain.

Wind will flow anticlockwise around a low pressure area. If you look at the synoptic chart above you will see that the wind direction is actually biased slightly inward toward the centre of the Low - rather like water flowing down a plug hole. (These directions are only true for the Northern Hemisphere - in the Southern Hemisphere the flow is in the opposite direction).

The majority of the 'weather' is concentrated around the frontal zones, and to clarify the characteristics the illustration below shows a cross-section through each type of front.

A warm front is a simply the approaching warm light air sliding up over the denser cool air. It will first appear as high cirrus cloud a few hours before the front itself. This cloud gradually lowers and thickens into nimbo-stratus or strato-cumulus; these are rain clouds, and light rain will fall, growing heavier as the

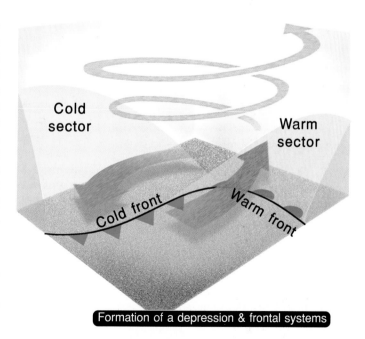

Formation of a depression & frontal systems

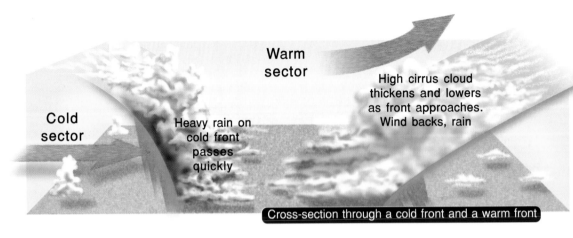

Warm sector

Cold sector

Heavy rain on cold front passes quickly

High cirrus cloud thickens and lowers as front approaches. Wind backs, rain

Cross-section through a cold front and a warm front

cloudbase drops. The wind 'backs' - that is, swings anti-clockwise, and strengthens. As the front passes over, the rain slackens, the cloudbase rises again and the wind 'veers' (swings clockwise, for example from south to west). Though you may not notice it, you will now be in a warm sector with higher air temperatures. The passage of a warm front from the first sight of high cloud can take many hours, so once the rain starts you can expect it to last a while.

A cold front is similar in that it 'shovels' warm moist air upward ahead of it, but looks quite different to the ground observer. The first signs are heavy rain, and possibly thunder, with cumulo-nimbus clouds on an active front. There may be a 'gust front' if the clouds are very large. This is an area of strong wind, which may extend some way in front of the clouds - this type of sudden wind can be very dangerous. As the front arrives, the wind increases and veers. After the passage of a cold front the cloud lifts quickly and the colder air may give a noticeable drop in temperature. Often, if the air is cold and the sun is shining this may lead to thermal activity inland soon afterwards with gusty winds.

Cold fronts can be more violent than warm fronts, because they travel faster and the warm air is pushed up more quickly. The whole front may arrive and be gone in a couple of hours, so if it is chucking it down when you arrive it may well be worth waiting..

High Pressure Systems

High pressure regions, or anti-cyclones, can be visualised as huge mounds of air, the additional weight of which is constantly sinking and flowing downwards and outwards, and which acts as a lid that prevents thermals climbing to form cumulus clouds.

The weather in the summer is often hot and may be humid with little wind. When a strong high is established directly overhead it may last many days, and unless a sea breeze occurs (see below) the windsurfing possibilities may be very limited, as the winds will be very light. However, if the high is off to one side of your region, it can result in a steep pressure gradient, when the opposite is true: the air is accelerated as it flows around the side of a high, and can give strong winds and clear skies.

In winter the trapped, warmer, more humid air can be cooled at night by contact with the cold ground and fog or mist is common on high pressure days.

Micrometeorology

Once we have the basic picture from the forecast, we must add some local detail; this is best predicted by being aware of the characteristics of the wind. It will tend to split around a headland, for example, but will be 'pulled in' to a bay with high ground around it.

When the wind is cross shore on any coast that is not straight, there will be areas of wind shadow behind promontories or any large obstacle, like a harbour wall.

In places where the wind crosses land before a stretch of water, the airflow will be affected by the factors affecting that land, such as thermals. A thermal is a bubble of air that is heated by a warm surface (like a town or a south facing slope). As the warm air expands and rises, nearby air rushes in to replace it, and the result is felt by the sailor as firstly a lull and then a gust of wind. Piled-up white cumulus clouds often mark thermals. The bigger and taller the clouds, the stronger the thermals. When conditions are good for this kind of convection the air is referred to by weathermen as unstable - and that is just how it feels.

Because air is affected by drag, and land is much rougher and therefore 'draggier' than the sea; the wind a few hundred metres offshore is very often stronger than close in. So if the wind is close to your limit for a specific sail size on the beach, it is likely to be more powerful a bit further out.

Sailors tend to look ahead, but it is worth looking over your leading shoulder to check what is upwind of you: gusts and stronger winds are marked by ruffled patches on the surface which always look darker, so you can anticipate approaching patches of wind (or lulls). The water surface is a good indicator of strength and consistency of the wind.

Even if it does not feel too strong where you are rigging, white caps or streaks or foam are a powerful indicator that it is blowing up out there..

Sea Breezes

These are an important feature of coastal weather. A sea breeze is formed when

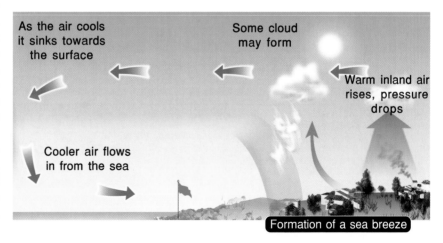

As the air cools it sinks towards the surface

Some cloud may form

Warm inland air rises, pressure drops

Cooler air flows in from the sea

Formation of a sea breeze

there is a light prevailing wind or none at all, and the general heating of the land creates a lot of convection as the arm air rises. The cooler air lying on the water then flows in to the low pressure area inland, and the breeze gradually swings more onshore and strengthens as the day progresses. In the evening, as the land cools more quickly than the sea, this process is reversed, so at dusk a sea breeze may die away quickly and as night falls a land breeze may develop (well worth knowing if you are sailing well out from shore on a sea-breeze day and its getting late…).

In many countries with warm climates this is a daily phenomenon, and the sea breezes are standard feature of many well-known coastal windsurfing venues. Even around the UK coast it can be as much as Force 3 and above on hot summer days, making apparently windless days quite usable to those in the right place.

A light onshore breeze can be reinforced by the sea breeze as well, making a day that seems a little too gentle inland, actually quite strong at the beach.

Wind Gradient.

On the most detailed level, the main characteristic of the wind is the fact that it gets stronger the further it is from the surface. This is of interest to us if we are lucky enough to have a choice of sailing venues, as a lake or reservoir at, say, 700ft. above sea level, will enjoy a stronger wind than the coast on the same day.

Sometimes there just isn't any wind! But that doesn't slow down the windsurfing women of Vassiliki!

Carve Gybing

No matter how good your tacks are, the act of pointing upwind will rapidly decelerate the board. If you enter a tack with loads of speed you can carve all the way around on the plane; but if you slow down too much your board will start to flounder and a low volume board will start to sink.

Gybing, however, can be performed at high speed, and done well it is achieved with grace and style and without com-

ing off the plane. No wonder mastering this exhilarating technique is the objective of every windsurfer.

Because it is a subtle combination of moves and happens quickly, carve gybing is also a technique that is challenging to get just right. Traditionally, the best way to tackle such a technical skill is to break it down into smaller pieces, practice each one, and then link them together. Carve gybing defies this logical instructional approach, as thinking too much seems to ensure failure!

The steps involved in the carve are laid out below; but success depends upon not only knowing the steps and understanding the process, but also in adopting a more zen-like approach, of mentally visualising the perfect carve gybe many times before you do it, and then 'going for it' in one fluent action.

Previous gybes will have been initiated by stepping back, sinking the tail of the board, scooping the rig and pressing on the outside rail to turn. From a planing position the requirements now change to keeping the board horizontal, steering with only the feet and pressing the inside rail to carve the turn! If you have been flare gybing for a long time you may have to de-program yourself to some extent to overcome your instinct to 'squat and scoop!

It is always helpful to go though the actions a few times on dry land (preferably on a simulator if you have access to one) to fix the sequence of actions firmly in your mind.

Preparation

Choose the right location. For your first carve gybes you need plenty of room, reasonably flat water so that waves or chop do not make it more complicated, and lots of speed! Many carves founder because the entry speed is too low. A key point here is that you only need to be actually carving from a broad reach to a broad reach, i.e. 90 degrees or so.. To try and carve from a beam reach to a beam reach the other way is 180 degrees and is far less likely to succeed without dropping of the plane..

Equipment

Do not combine a new technique with new equipment - you should be familiar with the kit you are using. However, carving is much harder on older long boards or on very small low-volume short boards. If you have a daggerboard, remove it completely - it is of no real use in the good planing conditions you will need. Choose a sail which will give you plenty of power.

Mental preparation is vital too. You must be positive about going for it, and expect that you will succeed! This manoeuvre needs to be tackled fearlessly!

There are an almost limitless number of variations to the gybe, but the two main techniques are the step gybe (when your feet are switched before the turn is completed) and the strap-to-strap gybe (when you do not change feet until you are sailing away on the new course). Both have advantages and disadvantages - the step gybe is little more stable and perhaps a little less demanding - the strap-to-strap gybe is potentially a bit faster and smoother, so it gives a better chance of staying on the plane.

Firstly the step gybe...

From a reach, bear away onto a (broad) reach and wait until you have reached maximum speed. Check that the area you are turning into is clear and the wind and water seem consistent.

You should have a relaxed, committed stance and the board should not be bouncing or skidding.

Shift your back hand well back on the boom.

It is important to keep sheeted in as you initiate the turn.

Slip your rear foot out of its strap and move it forward and closer to the leeward (inside) rail, with the toes pointing at the water.

Unhook! (but keep your hips forward and shoulders back.) Try not to disturb the equilibrium of the board as you make these preparations.

Pause a moment to ensure everything is feeling good, then go for it:

Lean forward and into the turn, pressing down with the toes of the back foot to start carving the board. As the board 'banks', go with it, staying upright relative to the deck, not the water!

Drive the board 'away' from you with your legs pushing the inside edge against the water, (particularly the rear leg) - this carves the rail and the board turns faster. Keep the boom away from you and the front arm extended. Sheet out more as the turn develops. Keep leaning forward.

Bring the back foot forwards as the board comes onto the new course. Swap your feet. Try to slide the feet around and not stamp. The sail will now be opened to the point where the clew is leading. Slide the old front hand closer to the mast clamp.

complete the dance.

This is the mechanics of a basic gybe. The key is timing and linking the moves smoothly. If the board slows and drops off the plane it doesn't really matter - just wind up your speed and try it again, perhaps keeping your weight a little further forward. It can take lots of practice, and may feel a little awkward initially, but the carve gybe is the key to mastering your kit at speed and is the basis for a whole raft of variations.

The strap-to-strap gybe...

The preparation and initial moves are the same, but the board is carved right around without taking the front foot from the strap. This means that the rig flip is done with the feet still pointing the 'wrong' way. To keep the board turning, the carving pressure switches from the toes to the heels, which are now controlling the new inside rail.

Flip the rig; make this a positive motion, throwing it around with the "old" back hand, then reaching underneath your new front hand to grab the boom, and bring the mast upright. Reposition the old front hand to the new back position.

Sheet in, and keep the knees bent as the power comes back on. Hook in, and slip your feet back into the foot-straps to

Laydown gybe

Duck gybe *(Photo: Gun)*

This means you are unsupported for a moment as your body is twisted with the heels pushing one way and your torso facing the sail as you flip the rig. This is a fast, smooth way to carve gybe, but is less suitable for slower or semi-carving turns. It is also less useful on longer, less agile boards.

As the board takes up the new course the front foot simply pivots out of the strap and slides straight over and into the new strap in one motion.

These are the basic steps, but as mentioned at the outset, the key is to try and reach a state where you are not counting down the moves, but are reacting automatically. For this reason lots of practice (both physical and mental) is required. It is all too easy to survive a gybe by getting it wrong and then 'learning' to repeat the same mistakes. A very useful exercise is to initiate a carving turn when on a fast beat, then swerve back up wind again. After a few sweeping S turns, you will become more confident to go for it.

Variations

A carve gybe can be performed in several ways, either in technique or location.

Techniques include the laydown gybe, which is a modification where the sailor lays the rig almost parallel to the water, de-powering it momentarily and allowing a very fast turn. This is often used in racing or simply for extra style.

The slam gybe is a technique similar to a high speed flare gybe, where the board is pivoted around the fin in a very tight arc, almost on the spot, before powering up again on the new course. Also useful in some race situations or in restricted space.

The duck gybe is a variation with no particular function except the 'look at me mum' factor. The clew is thrown over the sailor's head (he is, of course, ducking) instead of being flipped over the nose.

The location can be changed too; the early gybes should be performed on flat water for the best chance of success, but gybing on waves introduces a whole new set of challenges and rewards. Gybing on the face of the wave or 'off the lip', where the nose of the board may be in mid-air and almost vertical is a favourite manoeuvre of expert sailors.

Gybing around a mark in races demands excellent control and navigation. And for those into big air, the ultimate change of direction can be performed in mid-air!

Or with one hand! *(Photo: Bic)*

Waves

Dealing with Waves

Many people learn to windsurf on flat water, such as a lake or reservoir, or on a sheltered bay in the Mediterranean or the Red sea. But as you progress to planing in stronger winds, or buy your own kit and venture out to the beach, you soon start to encounter waves. The mix of strong wind and water always produces some small waves, and dealing with this low chop is often simply a matter of flexing the knees a bit to keep the board flat.

Ocean swell

In force 4-5 winds the swell breaks. "White horses" appear

The wave encounters the bottom and is pushed up into a shore break

lines of breakers. If it is coming straight at the shore, and the sea bed is the right shape and angle, the waves can grow to massive proportions. In shallower approaches, or with the beach at an angle to the swell, the waves can lose much of their energy and height before they arrive. With a little knowledge and experience, and knowing the tides for their local beach, sailors soon become adept at forecasting the likely height and power of the waves at their local spot. (More information on tides is given in Chapter 6.)

When you venture into deeper water, or sail the coast of a larger sea or ocean, the waves change character. The surface of the water has had time to react to the pushing of the wind to form a swell - the typical heaving surface of the sea. The height of the swell depends on the wind strength, how long it has been blowing and the 'fetch' - the distance the uninterrupted wind has had to develop the swell.

A storm hundreds of miles away can start this process, and the bigger the ocean, the bigger the potential for swell. If a swell gets too high (in fact, more than one seventh of the distance between peaks) it will start to break and form whitecaps. This starts to happen when the wind reaches force 4 or about 15mph.

The real fun starts when the swell approaches the land and is resolved into

Beach launching in a shorebreak requires a good technique and good timing to pick the right moment. The board is very vulnerable, being controlled by only the mast foot pressure, and you are well advised to carry the board and rig together if you can, and drop the board into the right position, stepping on without delay.

Rather than the most comfortable position sandwiched between the board and rig, it is worth the effort to carry them into the water both held on the downwind side. If you lose control you will not get "scissored" between them.

As soon as you are on board, sheet in to get moving - you need some momentum to climb over the first wave, which you should 'take' head on. Some wide boards have very long fins and you will need to get your foot up to above waist level in the surf to start. This requires plenty of practice, as it is really the latter half of a waterstart. In big waves you will need a wave board!

Do not commit to the straps too early - you may need to move forward to help the nose pitch over the crest of the wave.

Getting out into the waves is only the start: if you fall off (and you will), it is far harder to up-haul in a rolling swell. The best advice is to be practised at waterstarts before taking on big waves.

Getting out of the water in waves is also a potentially hazardous manoeuvre. Use the power of the waves to surf in to the beach, but slow down as you reach shallow water, so that the wave breaks ahead of you. It is better to sail right in on the foam, then step off quickly to avoid a wave dumping water onto your board from behind. Do not drop your rig in the surf, but step off smartly and lift the tail of your board to protect the fin as you push it quickly into the shallows. Get the whole issue out of the waves as soon as possible.

Going for it: Wave Sailing

Windsurfing offers a wide range of challenges, and you have never finished learning. However, some sailors do find that once they have nailed blasting at speed, carve gybing and a few interesting variations, their sailing is becoming a bit jaded.

After all, the best fun and sense of achievement is from mastering the things you cannot do, rather than repeating the things that you can!

There are a number of paths the competent sailor can follow: some will compete, some will gain satisfaction from passing on their knowledge as instructors and some will continue to seek new challenges. In windsurfing, the most interesting and challenging environment is undoubtedly sailing in waves.

Waves can appear be a random swell in deep water, offering an ever-changing surface to sail on or to act as a ramp for jumps. However they do follow a pattern, and are usually arranged in sets of larger waves followed by an area of relatively flatter water. They resolve themselves into regular sets of breakers as they encounter the bottom and roll in towards the beach. This can give exhilarating conditions for surfing down the face, gybing off the lip, or launching into the air.

Breaking waves and white surf are a mix of air and water, and as such they have slightly different characteristics to the

flat blue stuff. You will need to be adept at water starts as uphauling will be impossible. You will also need a very agile and reactive board to allow sharp changes in direction. Your rig must not only be easy to manage but will also need to be tough to take the inevitable pounding when you wipe out and a ton of water lands on it. A small board and rig means you will need plenty of wind, of course, so you will need to master all these factors. Plenty of new challenges there, then!

The Kit

All manufacturers offer a small wave board, built for slashing up the face and easy jumping and landing. They are agile and tough, and the lack of area at the tail means they also absorb some of the landing impact when you do splash down.

The big, wide early planing boards are a huge disadvantage in waves, where the wind can get under the nose and shove them around, and the big fins are subjected to huge pressures as you pivot or land on them. There is no way around it - if you want to really get into wave riding you need a wave board.

Sails are almost as critical; small, agile tough sails with a high cut foot will make life much easier in waves. If you have been using a seat harness, hooking in and out becomes a bit of a drama; all wave sailors choose waist harnesses for this reason.

Often only seen in cold weather on flat water, helmets are a must in waves, where the chances of your head making contact with your own kit (or someone else's!) are massively increased.

Wave sailing and the jumps that are an integral part of it are a real test of skill and control; the advanced techniques required are constantly evolving and are beyond the scope of this book. However, top sailors are typically very generous with their advice.

Articles in the windsurfing magazines are always packed with informative tips on the latest tricks and techniques.

Photo: Bicsport

Big waves demand respect! (Photo: Gun,

Packing, Transporting & Care of Your Equipment

Packing & Transporting

When you have finished sailing for the day, your board and sail are likely to be wet or sandy or both.

Rinse off any sand before leaving water if practical; allow a few minutes for it to dry and find a clean area to pack it up. In areas with sharp rocks, mud, or blowing sand and with and nowhere else to pack, some sailors choose to roll up the sail in the water and dry it later at home.

Removing sand and seawater helps prolong the looks and useful life of your sail, as the particles of sand and even the crystals of sea salt will gradually scratch the monofilm and abrade the fabric. This process is accelerated with lots of movement, so the sails should be rolled into a tube and secured in a sail bag as soon as possible. Never leave an unrigged sail flapping in the breeze.

A few sails may require a batten to be removed, but generally the sail can simply be rolled, starting at the head and rolling parallel with battens down to the tack. On some larger sails the top portion may need to be folded once onto the body of the sail to line up the battens before rolling.

A sail should never be squashed flat if avoidable (by having heavy objects laid on top of it, for example, or being crushed into a roof-rack by a strap). Creasing the monofilm will weaken it and reduce its ability to assume a smooth clean foil in use.

Ideally, sails should be transported inside a vehicle or tied down firmly but without excessive pressure.

Boards are extremely tough in many ways, but they are also easy to scratch or damage by knocking them on a sharp object like a small rock (or the corner of a car door!)

When taking your board out of the water, take care to place it so that it will

A perfect rigging and de-rigging area. This is Rutland Water, UK.

If it travels on the roof, get some padding around the rack bars. You can buy purpose-built pads from most watersports shops, or regular pipe lagging from a DIY store will also work perfectly.

It may seem obvious, but it is much better for the board to travel upside down on the roof, so that the nose is curved down towards the screen and the fins are pointing upwards.

not be blown around, and never leave it within range of the surf. This is particularly important in tidal areas, where the tide has a nasty habit of sneaking in and floating your kit away or whacking it on the rocks while you are getting changed, sorting out your sail or regaling your mates with stories of your day's exploits!

Always rinse off any sand sticking to your board, and if you are transporting it in a bag, try and let it dry before packing it up. If the board is going inside a car, make sure it cannot flop around or has anything sharp near it. It is always worth spending a few minutes removing the fin in this situation.

In this position the fin (and your head) is less likely to get damaged as you get stuff out of the back of the car. With many hatchback or estate cars, the tailgate will swing up with quite a lot of force when it is opened The nose-down position on the roof also means that the airflow at speed is pushing the board down onto the rack. If the board is tied nose up, the lifting force will be trying to rip it off as you drive, and will put a lot of strain on the straps or ties holding the board down.

Trailer with padded bars for boards and booms and lockable box for sails and masts

Windsurfing gear is light and it is surprising how much will fit on a hire car *(Photo: Gun)*

The key to tying down kit is to ensure it is immobile. A surprising number of people tie down their boards with a single rope of strap that passes under the rack bar at one point. This is not sufficient. The straps should be long enough to pass over the board twice and be passed under the rack bars on both sides.

The perfect solution is to buy a camper van or (if that idea doesn't go down too well) some sailors have set themselves up with a trailer to transport and store their kit in perfect comfort!

Masts are very tough, but they can split if a heavy load is placed on them or a car tailgate is closed on the end! A good tip is to always slip them into the sail or board bag. Always remove mast extensions before putting them on the roof, as the vibration can loosen seemingly tightly locked parts. Many windsurfers carry a small holdall or box to store all their mastfeet, UJs, Grunts, spare bits of line and tools.

Dealing With Damaged Kit

If you should be unlucky enough to damage your board, how you deal with it depends upon the material from which it is constructed. Whilst some minor damage to glass-fibre skins is possible to repair at home, anything that fractures the outer casing of the board and allows water to reach the foam core is going to need expert attention. A variety of different materials are used to construct boards, and each needs different techniques and materials to repair; the best advice is to take it to a windsurf or surf shop, where an experienced member of staff can advise you.

Never sail a board with crack in it (other than back to shore!) as the larger the area

As long as the foam core is dry, you can clean, sand & 7 fill it. You can buy "ding" sticks of epoxy filler at most windsurf or surf shops.

Digging out the wet stuff (note the specialist tools!)

Glassing

Sanding

renewed by hand; however, the material is very tough, and to make new needle holes you will require a sailmakers 'palm' (a leather device to ensure the needle goes through the sail instead of your hand!)

You must only use waterprooof (polyester) thread.

A temporary alternative to stitching a small area (like a batten pocket) is to stick on a patch of sailtape. This is self-adhesive ripstop, mylar or polyester tape and

of foam that gets soaked, the larger the amount that will have to be replaced and the bigger the repair job will be.

If the foam is saturated, the only solution is to dig all the wet stuff out, and then rebuild the core with new EPS foam. (Kits with the correct chemicals preloaded into hypodermics are available from most windsurf stores).

The alternative, of course, is to have the repair done professionally.

For sails, small areas of stitching can be

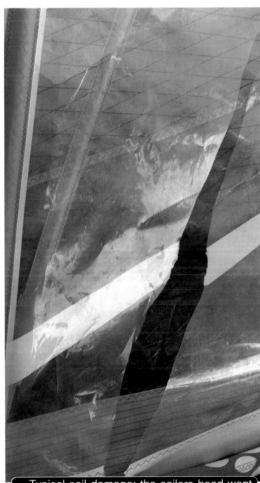
Typical sail damage: the sailors head went through, and the sail has spilt across several panels. A write-off

is very effective if properly applied to a dry surface. Repair tape is available from most windsurf stores or chandlers.

If using this tape, always round off the edges and rub it hard (using a coin works well) to ensure a secure seal at the edge.

Many sails are made of monofilm, and as it has no fibres, damage tends to split the sail right across a panel. The only solution is to insert a whole new panel, which is a job for a professional sailmaker.

Travelling

A padded board bag is a good idea to store and protect your gear, and is vital if you are travelling on a plane, train, etc., where your kit will be treated as baggage. If this is the case it is obviously necessary to remove the fin completely.

It also makes it much easier to carry everything, as booms sails and 2 piece masts can also be fitted into most bags, though you may need to add a bit of additional padding in places.

All airlines have baggage allowances, and these are often strictly enforced, especially on budget airlines. However, a stuffed board bag is far too large for the regular luggage conveyor, and it is common to have a flat charge for an oversized item, regardless of weight. For this reason, windsurfers often like to put as much kit as they can into one bag, and you can purchase double-depth bags if you are shifting a lot of gear, or if a couple of you are travelling together. Do plan ahead - it is no good turning up at your destination airport with a bulging board bag to find that the local taxis are all Fiat Unos with no roof racks.

If you are on a package, try and swing it with the rep. Before you leave to get a space for your kit on the bus; or if you are travelling independently pack a few spare straps!

Fortunately, taxi drivers in most well known windsurfing areas like the Canaries or Egypt are well used to heavily equipped travellers and (for the right tip) can lash your kit to the roof with practiced ease!

Accidents do happen and kit does get lost or damaged, so always ensure you have

'Just one small bag of clothes - oh yes - and this as well...

travel insurance that specifically covers the windsurfing risk and insures your kit for a realistic amount. Very often the cover offered by high street agents is not adequate.

You should make a quick visual check of your gear an integral part of your daily preparation. ALWAYS check your UJ by tugging the mast foot after it is connected: losing your rig is no joke, and probably means you will need to be rescued.

While you are at it, ensure your fin is secure and your outhaul and downhaul lines are in good condition and tied or cleated securely.

A periodic check of other items, such as the base of the mast and the fin box for cracks, and the sail stitching and batten pockets for wear are also useful, especially if the kit has been stored for a while. If you have a daggerboard, ensure it is moving freely.

Finally it may well be worth marking your stuff with your name and phone number. Stolen kit does sometimes get recovered, and boards do get washed up or collected by fishermen or coast guards! It may also deter thieves in the first place.

Don't even think about nicking it!

The RYA & the FastFWD Scheme

The RYA (Royal Yachting Association) is the official governing body of many recreational boating and water sports in the UK, including windsurfing.

There is a well structured and effective training programme, from absolute beginners up to advanced instructor level, and a key benefit of membership is the automatic 3rd party insurance cover for windsurfers.

Insurance cover of this type is a mandatory requirement when sailing at all clubs and most inland waters in the UK.

The RYA also offers technical and legal advice and represents our interests to landowners and government.

It produces many fine publications on all its activities, including windsurfing, and has expert staff who promote the sport, accredit training centres and organise courses for instructors.

Full details of the RYA can be found at the their website at www.RYA.org.uk., or by contacting them on 02380 604100.

At the time of writing (July '04), the windsurf rating system consists of 5 levels - these are summarised below. This is a linear progression, and has functioned very well for many years on the 'get one thing right before progressing to the next' school of thought.

...structor Ali, runs through the basic moves with his (first) Fast Fwd class..

Level 1: Learn to Windsurf.

Practical:

Attain an appropriate level of competence at:

- Carrying and launching the board and rig separately.

- Establishing the secure position.

- Coming ashore safely.

- Sailing across the wind.

- Upwind and downwind power control.

- Steering - sailing a triangular course, turning the board, basic tacking and gybing.

- Rigging from components, de-rigging and storage.

Theory:

- Anti-collision rules.

- Self-rescue and distress signals.

- Sources of weather information.

- Effects of tide.

- Choosing a sailing venue.

- The points of sailing.

- Towing a board, steering and sailing a course.

- Personal clothing and buoyancy.

- Equipment transportation.

- Insurance matters, clubs, the RYA and publications.

Level 2

As Level 1 plus:

Show an appropriate level of competence at:

- Beachstarting.

- Competent launching and landing of the board and kit.

- Improved stance and steering.

- Basic harness use.

- Sailing a triangular course.

- Tacking.

- Gybing, including tail sinking.

- Rigging the equipment.

- Understanding basic rescue and safety techniques.

- Sailing theory.

- Understanding sailing conditions.

Level 3

As level 2, plus:

Show a good level of competence and understanding at:

- Tacking in stronger winds.

- Gybing, including tail sinking, clew first sailing, and daggerboard up and down.

- Self rescue and dealing with emergencies.

- Planing.

- Waterstarting.

- Knowledge of the sail and rig, including

types and rigging.

- Weather assessment, including tides.

- Further theory, including apparent wind, upwind performance factors, and mast foot pressure.

- Harness types.

- Care of your equipment.

Level 4

As level 3, plus:

Show a good level of competence and understanding at:

- Tacking in stronger winds.

- Carve gybing.

- Improved water starting.

Level 5

As level 4, plus:

Show a good level of competence and understanding at:

- Gybe variations (Duck, Slam, etc.).

- Tacking low volume boards.

Start 'em young! *(Photo: Starboard)*

This system is currently undergoing a radical overhaul to bring it up to date with advances in equipment, and the emphasis is changing to embrace working from a formula of concentrating on fundamental core skills (Vision, Trim, Balance, Power control and Stance). By focusing on these skills, the actual exercises of getting planing and all the rest should come more naturally to the new sailor. And 'self coaching', which is the main route to improvement, becomes easier to manage.

In the past, these skills have sometimes tended to be acquired as a by-product of attempting the specific exercises, rather than the other way around.

The new coaching programme is called the Windsurfing FastFWD system. And is the culmination of many years of experience and coaching by the well-known coach Simon Bornhoft

The new syllabus consists of the basic Learn to Windsurf course (as the current Level 1), leading to a core skills course (the FastFWD course).

This will be the standard vehicle for mastering the core skills.

During this course, the practical skills will include board and rig set-up, planing skills, footstraps and harness use. This reflects the ease with which modern kit allows new sailors to start planing at a much earlier stage than before.

The fundamental principle of the new training system is to highlight the key areas common to most situations in windsurfing, rather than the actual physical techniques, so that the sailor can run through a 'self check' of each of the five key points at any time, and thereby help himself to make improvements.

To progress from the standard FastFWD course, there are several modular clinics available, each concentrating on different skills and aspects of the sport.

Good instructors have always taught the various skills with reference to the need for fundamentals, such as looking ahead, trim, power control, etc.

But by making these the focus of the training, rather than a by-product, it is hoped that the progress to higher levels of competence will be quicker and smoother.

So what is the fast forward formula and how is it applicable to the various stages of learning.

The five essentials are:

- # Vision
- # Trim
- # Balance
- # Power
- # Stance

Vision

This is the first element and is the first consideration when sailing. Where you are looking, and your position and course relative to the wind are the primary points to establish. This is critical to be able to maintain a course relative to the wind, (which may be changing in direction), and to ensure the area you are turning or sailing into is clear. There is another vital point to good vision as well, humans are very visual creatures and sight is our primary sense, looking the right way and positioning the head correctly, makes the other elements of balance, trim, power and stance are far easier to achieve.

For example if you wish to turn (either upwind or downwind) , look that way before initiating any actions, and you are more likely to succeed safely, and exit the turn on the correct course.

A common negative effect of vision being applied badly is gazing for prolonged periods at your sail, feet or hands. "Gear gazing" is bad news and is about as useful as looking at the gear lever when driving. i.e. handy for a quick glimpse, but not much more!

Trim

This term refers to keeping the board correctly orientated which for almost all the time means flat.

A flat board is more stable, holds a course better, and is faster than a tilted or angled board. If your board is not flat in normal sailing then something is not right and needs to be corrected.

A well-trimmed board is much more likely to hold a course, to get planing quickly, to allow you to use the footstraps or harness, and generally sail better.

So how is a good trim achieved?

It is primarily a result if good weight distribution, and application of the forces

Good vision: Head up and eyes on the course ahead

Good trim: The front foot is in line with the board, and the rear foot is across the board. The feet are shoulder width apart. Good stance, Vision, Balance and Power control complete the formula *(Photo: J Carter, Bic)*

from the rig and fin. In practice this means keeping your front foot pointing toes forward, and moving it fore and aft as required to apply pitch control.

Keeping your rear foot at 90 degrees to the board and using toe & heel pressure or moving your foot if required to apply side to side (roll) control

When harnessed in, using the harness to apply mast foot pressure to act as a "third foot" and help pitch control as well.

Footstrap positioning is also critical in affecting trim at higher speeds, and reflects the necessity for both feet to move back and outboard to balance the force of the rig.

The faster you sail and the smaller the wetted area of the board the more sensitive it becomes to trim input, and when blasting even the pressure of one toe is enough to affect your course and speed.

An example is when the board is on the point of planing, reducing weight on the rear foot to flatten off the board is vital to help the board make the transition to planing, this is achieved by leaning forward and out to "lighten" the back foot.

Balance

We first think of balance as being able to stand on the board, often in swell and shift our weight in order to stay upright! Because you are holding a boom and are either helping to support the weight of the rig or countering the force generated by the sail, balance becomes a question of keeping that weight and force away from your body. Essentially to maintain good balance you and the rig should never be in the same place at the same time, or moving the same way at the same time. Keep it away from you!

Balance is critical in maintaining that other essential "Trim".

In order to maintain rig and body separation and to create a flexible framework, the key skill is to extend the front arm. Of course there will be moments when this is not possible and you find yourself up close to rig (when hooking in for example), but the basic rule is to move away from the rig again as soon as practical and rebuild the balanced framework.

If the rig is moving in one direction, your

Unbalanced; boom too close to body

The power of the rig well balanced against body weight

body should balance it with an equal and opposite reaction. As the sail pulls harder forward, you lean out and move back, as you move the rig backward you lean further forward. If the rig is moved across the board your body needs to move the opposite way.

Power

Power management is possible in two ways. The first is almost impossible to separate from balance and stance, as is it is the action of moving your weight down and out or backward to control the sails' power. The more obvious method and the one that this element of the Fast fwd formula is concerned with, is sheeting the sail in and out.

As explained in earlier chapters, the sail's power is a result of its angle of attack, and by lowering the angle (sheeting out), we reduce the power, this is also possible by sheeting right in on a broad reach for example. If the rig is balanced and the board is trimmed, the sailor can manage the power simply by extending or flexing the rear arm to set the sail to the correct degree to control the power. It is worth noting that the sail works best if disturbed as little as possible, and speed and power will be maximised by finding the "sweet spot" for the rig and managing the power primarily through balance, trim and stance.

To manage power through sheeting in and out you do need to have the boom at the right height and if hooked in, your harness lines must be in the right position. You need to be holding the boom in the right place (usually with the hands about shoulder width apart).

Stance

The position of the sailors' body is a vital element in successful control.

There are a few basics to achieving a good stance, and some of these are integral to the vision, trim and other elements of the Fast Fwd formula.

Keeping the head up and facing where you are going, having the feet in the correct position as discussed in the section dealing with Trim, and holding the boom at shoulders width and with front arm extended, with the harness lines set up correctly.

In addition to this, a good stance requires a straight back, hips forward and shoulders back, the legs should be fairly

The Standard 7 stance

'Drop and Dig' or 'Super 7' stance *(Photo: D Eberlin)*

straight for straight line blasting (especially the front leg). This basic position is the standard "Straight 7" stance. (See pic on the previous page).

It is almost inevitable that a new sailor will find themselves countering the force of the sail by sticking their backsides out and leaning forward. This position is almost guaranteed to give you backache, so adopting a good stance as soon as possible is a key skill. Using a harness helps enormously in this respect.

By holding your hips forward it supports your back and encourages you to lean back with your shoulders to balance the rig. The basics of the standard 7 stance. This position should be the aim whether or not you are in the harness

The power of the rig changes with the course being sailed, the wind strength and other factors and so the sailors' stance does have to alter to react to this.

As power increases it is often necessary to load the boom downward and outward to control the power and to do this the knees are flexed and the body weight is lowered and moved outboard as far as possible. (See pic above)

When trying to get planing in marginal conditions the stance can be modified by lifting the hips, locking the legs straight and loading the mast foot by leaning forward slightly. Your stance is constantly being altered to suit the conditions. By being aware of the basic "Lock and lift" to the standard 7 for speed; and the "Drop and dig" to the super 7 for power control, combined with the other elements of the Fast FWD formula, you are in a much better position to self-coach and improve.

Putting it all Together

The five elements of the Fast FWD formula are interdependent and it is of little use adopting (say) good vision with a poor trim. The final element : Stance, is to a great extent a product of the other elements all being in place. If you run quick self-check periodically, to ensure that your vision, trim, balance, power control and stance are all as they should be you will find the majority of common problems will be easy to identify and put right, your sailing should be faster, smoother and more comfortable, and you will look good too!

To progress from the standard Fastfwd course, there are several modular clinics available, each concentrating on different skills and aspects of the sport.

Carole (Team Bic sailor) pictured in 2003. She may never have heard of the Fast Fwd formula but she is demonstrating its's main elements anyway! - Good vision (head up and looking ahead). Good Trim with a flat planing board. Carole is well balanced with an extended front arm and good distance from the rig, and is leaning forward as the rig is raked back. Although her rear arm is straight his sail is well sheeted in, giving good power; mostly as a result of her good stance, the front leg is straight and the rear one flexed. Her hips are twisted forward holding the rig down and she is looking relaxed!
(Photo: Bicsport)

These include :

Speed

How to tune gear and body to get the best performance.

Waves

Techniques and equipment for wave sailing

Improving turns

Duck gybes, slam gybes, laydown gybes, carving tacks etc....

In addition to the changes in the training formula, the RYA has taken the opportunity to specify a much needed minimum level of modern boards, sail and other equipment an accredited centre must possess, including a new simulator.

Simulators have always been a helpful tool to enable the instructor to demonstrate and advise on new techniques, however they have always had a number of drawbacks as well, in that the feedback from the "rig" is not a reflection of the real

sensation of sailing. Though a wide variety of ingenious pivots and bungee cords tied to trees etc have been tried!

The new Fast FWD simulator is a requirement for a Fast FWD centre and whilst it does still suffer from many of the drawbacks of existing simulators should nevertheless help pupils familiarise themselves with the correct sequences and feel of an exercise under close supervision before getting wet!

All instructors are required to do conversion training to the new programme and be re-validated.

The Fast FWD programme will be gradually introduced over 3 years and

It should "raise the bar" for the standards expected of an RYA approved training centre.

The RYA also runs coaching/instructor courses and awards instructor qualifications. It recognises & accredits training centres that are equipped and teach to their standards.

Photo: D Eberlin

When the new system is fully functional; (The projected time scale for this is Jan 1st 2007) there will be three levels of RYA accredited centre.

- ### Start Windsurfing Centre
  Teaching beginners to the old level 1.

- ### Windsurfing FastFwd
  Running the new scheme including skills clinics.

- ### Advanced Windsurfing Fast FWD
  As above but with an advanced instructor capable of teaching to advanced skill levels.

The RYA are also active on the promotional front at club level, and although the competition circuit tends to be international in flavour the "grass roots" competition and especially youth windsurfing are well looked after by the RYA.

"T15" is the 15 years old and under initiative and comprises a network of clubs and competeitions that promote youth windsurfing, keen youngsters can get involved and can often use club kit if they have none of their own. The regattas and races are closely fought and are a brilliant way for your sailors to improve and enjoy their sailing, and in the company of their mates, rather than just with there mums and dads and the old fogeys at the sailing club! The T15 area (including message board) is found at the RYA website.

For further information about the RYA , membership, insurance, training schemes, accredited centres and instructor matters. Visit their website at www.rya.org.uk.

Photo: Starboard

Buying Your Equipment

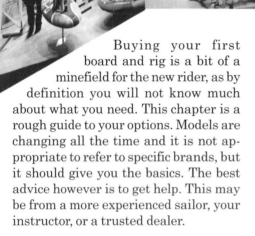

Buying your first board and rig is a bit of a minefield for the new rider, as by definition you will not know much about what you need. This chapter is a rough guide to your options. Models are changing all the time and it is not appropriate to refer to specific brands, but it should give you the basics. The best advice however is to get help. This may be from a more experienced sailor, your instructor, or a trusted dealer.

Many sailors with a few years under their belts may be very competent windsurfers themselves, but as change has been very rapid in recent years, and quite a few sailors use kit from only one manufacturer, they may not necessarily have a very wide knowledge of all the options for the new buyer.

If buying new, a dealer or instructor is usually your best bet, and the choice of excellent modern kit means that it is quite difficult to make a really bad choice.

When buying used, the story is a bit different. The boards last for many years and no-one likes to throw them away. The result is that there are literally thousands of old boards and sails out there, many of which are hopelessly unsuitable for a new sailor (despite what the owners might think!). So we will start with the easy bit!

Buying New

Boards

There are a bewildering variety of new boards in the shops and catalogues. Each manufacturer tries to have a model to fill every need, from high wind wave sailing to the broad formula boards aimed at planing in 8-knot breezes. Confusingly, these last models often look very similar to the beginner's models you are likely to want. So where do you start?

Opposite is a selection from the BicSport 2003 range.

The recent generation of superwide boards - an innovation started by Starboard - are now offered by every major board maker; they have changed the face of beginners' windsurfing in the last few years. Offering a stable and easy planing platform, these high volume, wide nosed models are the weapons of choice for many new sailors.

They have a high volume, often of 200 litres or more, so choosing the right size is not an issue for most buyers. Very light riders, previously badly catered for, are the only exception to this. Some forward-looking manufacturers are just starting to build scaled down versions of their beginner boards. It is well worth asking your dealer about these. These superwide boards are a bit less agile than their smaller brothers, but will give the occasional sailor good use for many years. They do plane remarkably well (with centre fins removed), and will take you a long way.

If you have done a bit already, are a generally competent and ambitious beginner with time to devote to the sport, or are pretty light (less than 75kg), you could skip this first step. For planing use and a bit more agility for a variety of sea conditions, the mid volume (120-160 litre) teardrop or 'no-nose' freeride types are a good choice. The problem here is that this class contains boards aimed at all levels up to very competent racers, so choose with care.

Features to look our for are :

Daggerboards

Those that have these are normally aimed at first time buyers. Boards with no dagger are intended for use primarily in planing conditions, and are hard to

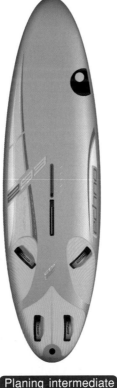

Beginner   Planing intermediate   Formula racer   Wave

sail upwind in light breezes, so only go for these if you are happy sailing upwind without one.

Footstraps

Most boards have a variety of footstrap positions; if you are not yet in the straps, make sure that they can initially be positioned fairly far forward and inboard, as this makes the transition much easier.

Decks

Eva foam decks are also a 'beginner' feature - good for early use, uphauling and comfort, but not as good as the rough non-skid surfaces for use in choppier water.

Size

The size you choose depends on your weight and the conditions you will be sailing in; most are available in at least 2 volume options.

Fins

A feature of many of these boards worth noting is the very long fin, which does make beach starting a little trickier. The water will need to be anything up to 70cm. deep to use one without grounding the fin.

Volume

The latest formula boards are also very high volume, so why not simply go for one of these? They tend to be lightweight and made of more fragile materials than a beginner's board; they do not have daggerboards and they are expensive. They are designed to work best with huge rigs and footstraps positioned close to the rails.

Wave-oriented boards are low volume, and therefore require a competent waterstarting technique and good strong winds to function. For these reasons neither type are suitable for the first time buyer.

Rigs

Wave sails tend to be small, tough, and have the foot set high to allow manoeuvring in tight spots, and to help keep them from being caught by white water breaking over the deck. These sails tend to be fairly flat in profile with a significant twist to favour manoeuvrability over power.

Race sails are built for ultimate speed and use a different airfoil section, and lots of battens, which rotate around the mast on camber inducers. The luff tube (the fabric pocket that houses the mast) is often wider to accommodate these and to minimise drag.

Race sails will feature a low-cut foot to minimise the gap between sail and board. Whilst all these features add performance, they also increase weight and cost.

Freeride sails are, as the name suggests, all round sails which give a wider range of use and are lighter and easy to handle. These are ideal for beginners. The range is enormous, and there are many 'hybrid' sails that feature characteristics of all these types

There are sails designed with a low centre of effort for those women or shorter men who prefer a lower boom position, and sails with few or no battens, designed primarily for children.

Sails come in a range of sizes, from tiny wave sails of less than 3 square metres, for use on tiny boards in howling conditions, to 12m. monsters that will drive a formula board onto the plane in even a

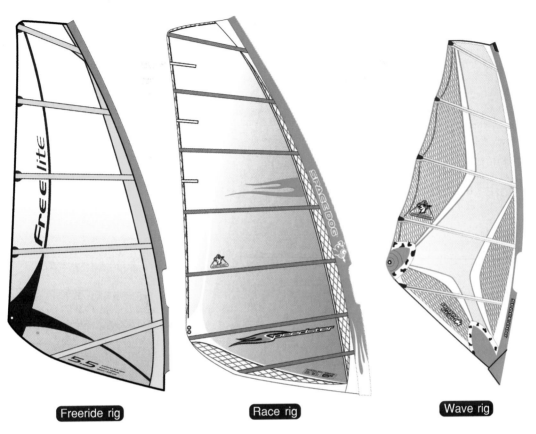

Freeride rig   Race rig   Wave rig

light breeze. Most beginners are well advised to use a sail in the 4.5-6.5m range to begin with depending on their weight and the wind strength. Too small and there is little power or resistance to lean against, too big and they are hard to handle and heavy to pull out of the water.

The size of sail you need depends on your body weight, board choice and likely sailing conditions. Assuming that you start with one sail, a very rough idea is that an 80kg. rider will probably need something in the 5.5-6m. range initially and a 65kg. rider would be looking a 4.7 - 5m. model.

Lighter sailors, particularly women, sometimes find up-hauling a physically draining activity, and many manufactures offer a very popular lightweight

range. Your dealer will advise you on the mast and boom to match the sail(s) you select. There is more information on sails in Chapter 8 that may help you make your choice.

If you are torn between sizes, go small! You will always have a use for it when the wind gets up!

Package deals

This is worth serious consideration. Trying to team an old board with a newer rig or vice versa is fraught with problems. By buying a package you get a better price and everything will be fully compatible. Packages of board and rig are definitely a good idea; the only point to look out for is that the masts are sometimes rather basic epoxy/ glass jobs that you will soon want to change. Choose a mast that is at least 25% carbon, as it will be lighter and last you much longer. (Most dealers will let you upgrade for the right price).

Price

It is worth looking around, but unless you can get a year-end sale or an ex-demo model, prices tend to be fairly consistent. Buying kit from the internet is certainly possible and can save you some cash if you know what you are doing, but many of the advantages of advice and back up from your local dealer will be lost.

You will probably need a wetsuit, harness, boots, gloves, etc., as well.

It is critical that these items are tried on before you buy: it can save a lot of hassle buying it all from the same place.

The same is true about buying from a supermarket. Decathlon, the sports megastore in France, does sell some branded (and some own brand)

windsurfing kit, and the price is noticeably lower than in the UK. However, the same provisos as internet shopping apply, and they will not be very interested in taking it back in part exchange when you want to move on!

Buying Used

A quick scan of the small ads in the windsurf magazines, the internet, or the local club notice board will yield an interesting variety of used equipment for sale.

Of course there is loads of perfectly good used kit out there, but be warned, a hairline crack from a being spanked with a boom or a de-laminating deck mat are not always easy to spot. Used beginners boards are quite likely to have been dragged up beaches and transported on car tops with no board bag. Sails may have batten damage, have been crushed or been fried in UV for many hours. Monofilm sails may be nearing the end of their useful life.

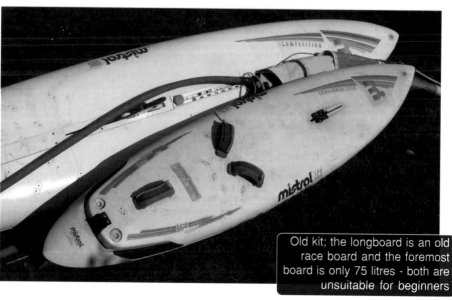

Old kit; the longboard is an old race board and the foremost board is only 75 litres - both are unsuitable for beginners

As mentioned above, any small and sinky boards (i.e. less than 120 litres) are clearly out of the question at this stage. Most of the rest will often be described as suitable for beginners; and to be fair to sellers, that is how it was probably described to them when they originally purchased it.

Before the advent of the modern designs featured in this book, which have only been really dominant since about 2001, the width and volume of boards were not the prime method of categorising them. Older boards were normally referred to as either long or short. A long board was anything more than about 320cm. in length. These had sufficient volume to allow uphauling, and featured a retractable daggerboard.

The basic rule was the longer the board the more 'beginner orientated' it was, and a typical starter board could be 350cm. or more. This type of board takes a lot of power to get planing properly and keen sailors soon found they were looking to change.

By the time you were down to 310s the feel was a lot less stable, but this kind of mid- length was where you were regularly planing, and where you learned to waterstart.

Short boards of this period, typically of 295cm. or less, were designed strictly for competent sailors, and are therefore not suitable a first time buy.

Between around '99 and '02 there was a kind of transitional period where the 320-ish boards grew noticeably wider, reaching about 80cm. in some cases, and these 'wide style' boards became very popular at training centres. Blow-moulded models from Bic, Tiga and Hi Fly are particularly common because of their excellent durability.

Unfortunately, early planing is not a strong point of this class, and although they are great for pootling around and family holiday use, they are not going to offer the keen sailor too much in the way of opportunities to progress.

What you buy depends on a number of factors - how much cash you can raise, how much you weigh, and what type of sailor you are.

The last point is a mixture of your fitness and attitude and how much training you have done. It is far better to spend a few quid on proper training at a centre with a range of modern kit before buying equipment that suits you at that point than it is to just buy first, and get your mates to teach you.

This way you are less likely to get it wrong; this is possible either if you 'undershoot', i.e. buy a huge board that you soon want to change, or 'overshoot' by getting a bit of kit you are not ready for. In either case, the eventual cost could be much higher than if you had had a bit of professional training and advice.

Buying used kit from separate sellers may have some compatibility problems.

Your mast may not suit the sail you have just bought, either because it is the wrong stiffness or length; length can be adjusted to some extent by the use of longer mast extensions, but some masts simply will not fit some sails. The same is true of booms: the mast-foot and deck-plate system may not be compatible. Check before you buy!

If you are changing boards, the same problems arise, and if you want to swap fins the situation is even worse, with four different fin-fixing options - none of which are compatible!

Even when it is all put together, a new-ish board will not show its full potential if teamed with an oldish sail, and (to a lesser extent) vice-versa.

Other Equipment

Which other items you will need depend on when and where you are sailing; these are discussed in Chapter 5. However, the most critical of these, and worthy of a closer look, is the wetsuit.

Even in water that you could happily swim in for several minutes, a wetsuit is a necessary piece of kit. The combi- nation of wet skin and wind acts to reduce the apparent temperature very quickly (see Chap- ter 12 for details of wind chill), and it is no fun sailing and very hard to learn while you are shiv- ering.

Wetsuits are available in a wide range of types to suit different tempera- tures. They work by trapping thin layer of water (or air) between your skin and the neo- prene. If the gap is too big, this allows water to drain away and be re- placed by a new batch of cold water, effectively cooling you down again. It is important that the

suit fits snugly and the entry points at neck, arms and feet are well sealed.

This does not mean they should be re- ally tight - a suit that limits the blood flow will also hasten cooling and can re- strict free movement. It is important that the suits are tried on and allow a good range of movement, so it is worth taking your time when buying.

Shorties: these have short (or no) arms, and leg sections down to mid thigh. Typi- cally made of 1 or 2mm. neoprene, they are useful to help maintain your core tem- perature in warmer water, and help com- bat any wind chill factor.

2mm shorty *(left)* and convertible wetsuit with arms off. *(Photos: Gun)*

The next level is a 3mm. suit with 2mm. arms and legs. Many of these are convertibles, featuring detachable arms, giving you some scope to regulate your warmth. 4mm. x 3mm. suits are slightly warmer again, and are useful for extending your range of conditions.

Cold water and fresh winds demand a thicker suit. And a 'steamer' with a 5mm. body and 3mm. arms gives a good level of warmth in most spring and autumn conditions. Suits of this thickness are often semi-dry, meaning they are designed to work with almost no water entry.

NB If it is really cold you will also need gloves and a neoprene hood. A good proportion of the body heat lost through wind chill is from your head.

Once in the shop and armed with a couple of plastic bags (to put on your feet to help slip the suits on), and knowing your likely sailing conditions, there is a still a huge variety of suits and prices. What should you be looking for?

The quality of the neoprene fabric. This determines the useful life of the suit - basically the stretchier the better. Most suits use less stretchy material in areas like the chest and very flexible types for underarms, lumbar areas and shoulders, that are in constant motion. Titanium layered neoprene is apparently more heat retentive and is used on some larger panels.

Fit and flexibility

The suit should fit snugly, especially in the lower back and crotch areas, and it should be easy to bend your knees and elbows without causing bunching, which soon becomes uncomfortable. If short armed, the suit should allow for a bit of bicep bulge as you are sailing.

The only area of the suit that can be very tight is the bit holding your belly in (for that James Bond look)!

The seams

Seams are usually one of three types: the first, flatlocked, is the 'conventional' stitching system that is comfortable, strong and economical, but it does allow some water through the needle holes in the seams. Flatlock seams are sometimes taped to reduce this - they are best suited to summer suits.

Glued and blindstitched seams are those where the needle does not pass right through the fabric, giving a fully waterproof seam.

Some recent models on the market are not stitched at all, but use a welding technique to connect the panels.

Water entry points: the sealing system at neck, ankle and wrist is very important, and winter semi-dry suits will use double seal systems. Neck seals can be very uncomfortable when the head is in constant motion - some kind of soft seal or flexible panel to minimise choke is a good idea - always try doing the suit right up and swivelling the head a few times to see how comfortable it is before buying!

Zips are the other main point of entry for water. As a general rule, vertical zippers are less waterproof than horizontal ones; new super stretchy fabrics allow many suits to have short zips or, in some cases, be completely zip free.

The neoprene is often laminated between layers of nylon; this makes it much more abrasion resistant and allows all sort sorts of colours to be added. However, the nylon does hold some water, which evaporates in the wind, draining heat, and so a smoothskin suit with no external layer is warmer, though easier to damage.

For this reason un-coated panels are often used in the torso area, and are combined with regular nylon-coated varieties for areas of higher wear, such as arms and legs.

Black suits are a bit boring, they all look the same, and make you much less visible in the water; so smooth suits are appearing with colours and logos printed onto the surface. Time will tell how durable this will prove on a stretchy surface, but the 'silver surfer' look is now one step closer!

Neoprene consists of a cellular material with the principal insulation coming from the gas trapped inside the cells. As the suit gets older the gas gradually escapes and the suit slowly becomes less efficient. This is an inevitable process and means that older second hand suits will have suffered a significant degrading of performance by the time they are about 5 years old.

If you are sailing in a shorty, 'surf slippers' will be fine for your feet. If the water is colder, you can get a reasonable seal at the ankle by using boots and ensuring the wetsuit overlaps on top of the boots to prevent water draining into them.

Your other purchases when setting up will be a harness and possibly a buoyancy aid and helmet. These items must be the correct size to be useful, so do try them on.

If you can get everything from one place you may be able to do a deal.... Remember that retailers have a profit margin on their stuff; so logically you are much more likely to get a 'free' board bag worth £40 with a board purchase, for example, than get a straight £40 off...(it's always worth asking anyway!).

Alternatively, safe a fortune on clothing by living somewhere hot! *(Photo: Starboard)*

Kitesurfing

You will not be windsurfing for long (at locations with a good beach anyway) before you come across kitesurfers.

Kitesurfing has grown very fast over the last few years, and many of those riders are also windsurfers as well. It is a brilliant sport, with its compact kit and relatively easy training programme, combined with the facility for big air and good speeds.

Compared to windsurfing, the sport does suffer from requiring a lot more room to set up and get going, and the upwind capability is strictly limited. The biggest drawback, however, is that if you ditch the kite in the water getting it airborne again can be a drama and take quite a while (sometimes it is just not possible, and you have to swim in and start over..).

Slashing down a wave, kitesurf-style! With very small boards and good flying characteristics, kites are becoming more and more common on good wave spots

If you are interested in having a go, do get lessons, and make sure that you spend enough time learning to master the kite and use the 'window' effectively before you try adding a board.

The basic steps to learn kitesurfing are:

- Choosing a good site and the correct wind

- Sufficient space, airflow over the landscape, wind strength and direction, hazards.

Photo: J8 Photograph

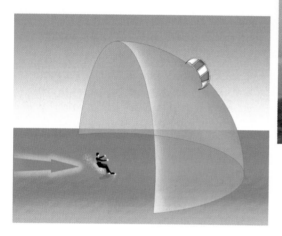

- Using a power kite

- Setting it up, knots, launch, basic control, emergency drop

- The window and the safe (zenith position). See below:

- Control, the harness and bar

- The sine wave pattern and de-power system

- The start and body dragging

- Using the kite in water with no board and learning to re-launch

- Introducing the board, starting in water, getting up

- Controlling speed, power and direction

- Learning to edge the board and make upwind progress

- Self-rescue and dealing with problems

- Packing up in the water

- Turning

- Usually just switching direction or stance on a twin tip board, or gybing on a directional board

- Beach starting, different kites, different boards, jumps

- Progressing to all the skills you will need to kitesurf safely in a variety of conditions and with others

Further information about learning kitesurfing are covered in detail in the sister book to this one: Kitesurfing, *The Complete Guide*.

Mixing it with Kitesurfers

In the earliest days of kitesurfing some windsurfers were less than happy at this new sport usurping bits of 'their' beach and sailing areas. A kite typically has 30m. lines and the idea of dozens of 30m. scythes zapping across the waves was a bit off-putting. In fact, kitesurfers favour big open spaces, so small reservoirs and bays where this may be an issue are rarely affected, and in any case the kite fraternity are, on the whole, very helpful and quite capable of hoisting the kite to the vertical zenith position if a windsurfer gets close.

Kitesurfers generally change direction by simply switching the kite toward the back of the board and riding the other way 'tail' first. This can be a bit unexpected if you are anticipating a gybe, so you do need to understand the patterns to sail safely with them.

There are possible conflicts, of course; any sailor (of either type) lying in the water is a bit of a hazard to other riders, and kitesurfers (like beginners at windsurfing) do spend quite a lot of time swimming!

The main issue is that in this situation the lines will be floating on the surface and are perfectly situated to catch the fin of a passing windsurfer. So vigilance is needed!

Kitesurfers have a lot less upwind capability than windsurfers, and this must be understood and taken into account when sailing in close proximity. But all of the anti-collision rules are the same and apply equally to both parties.

Kitesurfing is not part of the RYA in the UK, but has its own governing body, the British Kitesurfing Association (BKSA.).

Membership does give 3rd party insurance cover, so all kitesurfers in the UK should be members.

Like the PWA, there is a professional competition circuit, and the top riders are doing some very impressive freestyle tricks; there are local and national comps, too, which are well worth a look if you happen to be lucky enough to come across one.

If you arrive to sail and find there are kitesurfers also getting ready, the best bet is to go over and chat, find out whether they are beginners and what they are up to, and if necessary establish separate sailing areas. This kind of co-operation is a much better way forward than complaining about each other, and if you are lucky they might even let you have a go!

Frequently Asked Questions

Q Can I use my old windsurf board to kitesurf?

A Kiteboards are generally a lot smaller, they have the footstraps in a much further forward position, and they have harder rails for edging the whole board, rather than relying on a big fin. For all these reasons, converting an old board to kitesurf with is not a very feasible project, and the finished product still would not work very well...

Q Why are some kites 'bladders' that need blowing up and some foils like paragliders?

A Foils are actually far more efficient, but in the early days the re-launch capacity of bladder kites made them the only sensible choice. In fact, some foils are now quite re-launchable, and some of the bigger bladder kites are nearly impossible to re-launch in light winds, so the balance may be changing....

Q Why are some boards little wakeboard type things and others like a small wave board?

A Directional boards, very like a small wave board, were how everyone started; they go upwind much better and are easier to get going on. However, gybing one is reasonably skilful (similar to a windsurfing carve gybe), and the smaller twin-tips can be turned without any foot changes, so they are very appealing to beginners.

Added to that, the best tricks and biggest airs are easier with a tiny board and the twin tips are now very dominant.

(This does mean you can get a used directional board for next to nothing, however, and as a windsurfer you will find it natural to use)!

Competitions & Instructor Ratings

Windsurfing is a sport that almost everyone can enjoy, and many sailors simply get their pleasure from blasting around or playing in the waves. Humans are, however, naturally competitive animals - windsurfers more so than most - competitive, that is; not animals (well, with some exceptions..).

Even sailing solo is frequently a case of competing against yourself or the conditions, but when two or more sailors are sailing in close proximity, the focus of the competition becomes that bit more tangible!

Competitions run the full range from local club 'friendlies' to the professional circuit of the PWA, and all formats from freestyle to longboard racing. Many hard-fought competitions are in the youth categories.

There are many different options for competition; the thing they all have in common is that they are one of the driving forces for improvement, both in equipment and in personal sailing technique. At any level, a windsurfer can benefit simply from being overtaken by a better sailor.

Photo: D Ebberlin

Formula racing outfit *(Photo: Gun)*

Taking note of his stance, how his sail is trimmed, and the gear he is using all help you to improve your own performance.

Races can be triangular courses involving upwind beats and tacks as well as gybes. This type of course is favoured by the long board racers whose gear is tuned for maximum upwind performance and speed in all conditions.

Longboard racing is done on a 'class' board and sail, so that everyone is equally equipped; the boards are big (250 litres), and are designed to be used in all conditions, even in zero wind, where the riders must 'pump' their way round a course!

There are championships at national and European level, with the pinnacle of longboard racing being the Olympic event.

Fun board competition comes in a variety of flavours; the common element is that only planing conditions are used (though with the new formula boards that can mean as little as 8 knots).

Riders choose their own kit ,and as most competitions are run on production boards, the manufacturers have a lot riding on the results! The races may consist of a course with upwind and downwind legs and several laps to keep the spectators enthralled.

A common variation is slalom racing, which is essentially a downwind dash,

Natasha Sturges, GBR squad member (Photo: RYA)

Photo: D Ebberlin

strut their stuff with huge jumps and manoeuvres. These are judged on difficulty and style and the breathtaking skill of the top riders is truly incredible.

Loops, Table tops, Spocks and One foot Grubbies are the order of the day - not to mention the odd ariel dismount and major wipe out!

blasting at high speed and gybing around several markers. This is furious stuff with several sailors all gybing together at the mark.

Speed sailing is more of a time trial than a competition, being a straight sprint against the clock. Sailors take turns at completing a straight course in the shortest possible time, passing through a time gate at full bore and clocking their best speed over a measured distance. Technically, this is not a race, as it is done one at a time and the wind conditions can change, but it is certainly closely fought - huge sails and weight jackets are de rigueur for the serious competitors - with top speeds of over 40 knots being achieved by the very fastest sailors chasing the world record (currently held by Finain Maynard at a shade over 46.5 knots, or 53mph.).

The most spectacular competitions of all are freestyle wave comps, where sailors basically

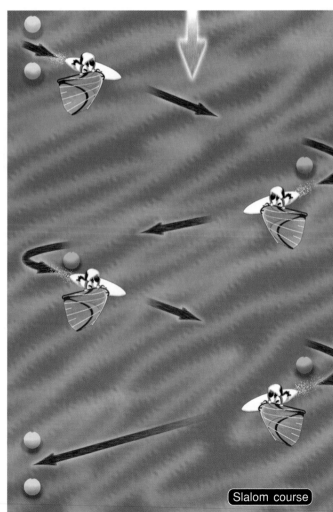

Slalom course

The interesting concept of indoor wind-surfing, which first came to prominence in Bercy, Paris, in 1989, was revived in 2004 at the Schroders London Boat show. Competitors slide down a ramp into the teeth of a 30-knot wind generated by a rank of huge fans, and blast their way round a very tight course (taking care not to hit the wall) and over the finish line in the shortest time. A jumping ramp was also included for some freestyle action (all you have to do is ensure your fin hits the slot in the ramp!) Add a few laserbeams and a good heavy rock soundtrack, and you have a fun-packed spectacle.

Actually the 2004 competition was dogged with technical problems: the fans were rather close to a back wall, and the airflow around the pool was chaotic, making a successful gybe a rarity. But the basic system has great potential and if someone would just move the walls of the building to allow a clean airflow, the sport could be a huge step forward for the publicising of windsurfing.

Going for it at the indoor comp at the London Boat show *(Photo: Dave Ebberlin*

The giant TV screen means that you can watch yourself as you slam gybe in front of it - surely a handy teaching tool!

Instructing

When you have been sailing for a while, and are pretty competent, ready for a summer (or winter) in the sun and would rather work in Turkey than selling turkeys in the local supermarket, the idea of becoming an instructor might appeal.

The bad news is that it appeals to a lot of people, so you do need to be a good instructor to get a job, and the pay when you do get there is (very) unlikely to make you rich. Only a very few instructors go on to owning their own businesses and making a good living from the sport.

So how do you get qualified?

Assuming that you are a reasonable sailor (you do not have to be a hero, just comfortable on the water), the next step is to attend an instructors course. In the UK these are offered by the RYA at regular intervals. You will learn the skills of teaching, how to use the instructor's 'tools' such as demonstration, question and answer techniques, etc.

Instructor Jason takes a waterstart clini

The actual gear, like simulators and a variety of kit, and perhaps techniques like video replay will need to be mastered. You will certainly have to show reasonable competence at handling a rescue boat, usually a RIB inflatable with an outboard. (An RYA Level 1 boat handling certificate is the minimum level.)

Obviously you need to be up to speed with your theory, and be able to explain the centre of lateral resistance or apparent wind with confidence.

If all goes well and you pass your instructors ticket, you can use it to help you try for a job at a UK centre or a holiday company that offers windsurfing.

Windsurfing is a great activity for just about everyone and teaching it is a very rewarding way of life *(Photo: Starboard)*

Many of the latter will be more likely to take you if you have a related skill, such as dinghy sailing, ski-boat driving or board repair experience.

If you have been teaching for a while and your own sailing is at least a level above the skills you wish to teach, you could apply for a rating to train an advanced skills clinic. Details of requirements for these will be available from the RYA as they are finalised.

The key requirement for an instructor is to be a good communicator and be able to make a wide range of people (including kids) feel comfortable with your input. This is far more important than simply being an ace sailor yourself.

Useful Contacts & Information

National Associations and Governing Bodies

International governing body: www.internationalwindsurfing.com

UK. Royal Yachting Association (RYA): www.rya.org Tel: 0845 345 0474/5

United States: www.uswindsurfing.org

Ireland: www.windsurfing.ie

Australia: www.windsurfing.org

Germany: www.dwsv.net

France: www.aff.net

Thailand: www.windsurfingthailand.com

New Zealand: www.windsurf.co.nz

Hong Kong: www.windsurfing.org.hk

Competitions

UK Windsurfing Competitions: www.ukwindsurfing.com

Professional Tour: www.pwawordtour.com

International Funboard Class Racing: www.internationalwindsurfinhg.com

UK Student Association: www.studentwindsurfing.co.uk

UK Weather

UK forecasts: www.bbc.co.uk/weather www.met-office.gov.uk

UK inshore waters: www.bbc.co.uk/weather/ship-inshore.shtml

Wendy Windblows Coastal Stations (subscription service): www.wendywindblows.com

USA Weather

wwww.windcall.com

French & European Coastal Forecasts

www.meteo.fr/marine/cote

Tidal Data UK

www.tidetimes.co.uk   www.uktides.com

Tidal Data US

www.tidesonline.com

Tidal Data Worldwide

www.ukho.gov.easytide.html

Photo: Gun

windsurfing

Talk to the experts - visit the tushingham website for a full directory of windsurfing shops, schools and locations with links to all the best windsurfing sites.

www.tushingham.com

COMMITMENT • QUALITY • DESIGN

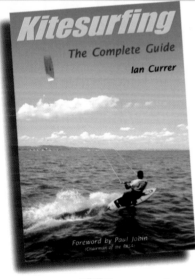

Kitesurfing
The Complete Guide
Ian Currer

Foreword by Paul Jobin
(Chairman of the BKSA)

This really is a comprehensive guide, covering everything from the history of the sport to innovations in the future - from what is involved on your very first days training, to competitions or becoming an instructor yourself. The book is laid out progressively using all the elements of a typical training programme.

Kitesurfing, The Complete Guide is endorsed by the British Kitesurfing Association and includes a foreword by Paul Jobin, the Association's chairman.

Available from all good bookstores or by phoning 0870 123 2555

£14.99

Glossary

Ariel

Any manoeuvre that is performed in the air.

Air

'Getting air', 'Big air' are terms of approval for big jumps.

Apparent Wind

The wind felt by the windsurfer and rig, a combination of the true wind and the airspeed induced by the forward motion of the board. See Chapter 15.

Aspect Ratio

A formula for describing a shape. A high aspect ratio sail, or fin, is tall and narrow - low aspect is short and broad.

Asymmetric

Some boards were originally a different shape each side for sailing a specific wave location. Now rarely seen.

Backside

The lee (downwind) side of a wave.

Backward Loop

Freestyle aerial manoeuvre!

Backwind

Sailing backwinded is with the wind and rig pushing toward you, not pulling away. Often done in freestyle moves.

Bale Out

Term for making an exit from your board in midair!

Battens

The stiffeners that support the sail, made of glass fibre or carbon. Usually tapered towards the mast, so that they bend more at the nose to form an airfoil shape.

Beach Start

Stepping straight on from the shore. The only practical way to start a low volume board.

Bearing Away

Altering course further downwind.

Beating

Sailing upwind.

Beaufort Scale

he nautical measurement of wind speed, divided into units from Force 1 to force 12.

Blasting

General term for planing at speed in the footstraps, and hooked in.

Blind Stitch

Blind stitching is used to join panels of a wetsuit without the needle piercing right through.

Blow Moulding

A manufacturing process used to produce relatively low cost and tough boards , though heavier than composite construction methods.

Bottom Turn

Wave sailing manoeuvre involving turning at the bottom of a wave to ride up the face again.

Broad Reach

Sailing on a course more downwind than upwind. The fastest point of sailing.

Buoyancy Aid

A flotation device that, er, aids buoyancy. Useful when learning.

Camber

The curve of an airfoil; in our case the shape of the sail when loaded.

Camber inducer

A plastic device at the end of the batten which sits against the mast. This helps the sail adopt its curved shape, and also helps it flip around the mast in a turn.

Carve

Carving a turn or carving a gybe is a way of altering course at high speed by banking the board into the turn.

Catapult

A spectacular means of dismounting, where the sailor is flung straight over the front of the board.

Centre of Effort (CE)

The balance point in the sail through which the power of the sail can be said to be acting.

Centre of Lateral Resistance (CLR)

The pivot point of a board about which it turns. This can be near the daggerboard, or, on daggerless boards, it is at the fin.

Chop

Small waves.

Chop hop

Getting the board airborne momentarily as you plane over chop.

Cleat

A small jamming mechanism that holds cords or ropes in one direction used on the outhaul and downhaul lines.

Clew

The outer or back corner of the sail, which attaches to the rear end of the boom.

Clew-first

Sailing along with the clew pointing forward.

Close Hauled

Sailing upwind with the sail sheeted well in.

Composite

Composite construction is the more expensive method of board production. It produces boards that are light, stiff and reasonably durable.

Convertible (Wetsuit)

One with removable arms.

Course Racing

Racing around a course in moderate to strong winds involving upwind and downwind legs.

Cringle

The metal grommet found at the tack and clew of the sail.

Cross-Shore

A wind blowing parallel to the shoreline. Also called sideshore.

Dacron

A woven polyester sailcloth., used in luff tubes and high wear spots of sails.

Daggerboard

The large, pivoting and removable 'fin' in the middle of a long or mid-length board.

Deck Plate

Connection to the board into which the mast foot is clipped.

Dehydration

Suffering from lack of water, (inside). If you are thirsty you are already getting dehydrated. It is common when physically active in a hot environment.

Downhaul

The downward tensioning system to set a sail; a huge amount of pressure is required to bend modern masts and a 6:1 (or more) pulley system is required to operate the downhaul effectively.

Duck Gybe

Advanced form of gybing where the sail is passed over the head.

Dumper

A wave that breaks suddenly on a steep shoreline, sometimes with a strong undertow. Hard to deal with and potentially bad for your kit.

Easi-rig

Trade name for downhaul handle, usually referred to as a 'grunt'.

Epoxy Resin

A substance used in the production process to bind materials. You can buy small tubes of epoxy in which the two elements are mixed to form a tough material, used to repair dings.

EPS

Expanded polystyrene, used for the core of most composite production boards.

Fin Box

The plastic cassette into which the fin slots. There are several types.

Flare Gybe

Turning the board by sinking the tail and pivoting the board around it.

Foot

The area from the clew to the tack along the bottom of the sail.

Footstraps

Straps to put your feet in so that you stay connected to the board at speed or in chop.

Freeride

General term for recreational intermediate boards and sails, i.e. those that are commonly used by most sailors for blasting around.

Freestyle

Tricks and manoeuvres on a board. This term used to encompass mostly light wind tricks, such as rail riding or helicopter tacks or riding backwards. But modern freestyle competitions have reached the level of tricks like double forward loops and spocks...

G10

Tough material used for fin production.

Glass fibre

Glass mat is cured with epoxy resin to form the hard outer skin of a board. Also called GRP.

Gnarly

Challenging conditions.

Grunt

General term for Easi-rigg, Rig Pulla or other downhaul device You can of course use a harness bar or anything handy to do the same job.

Gybing

A downwind turn that involves flipping the rig.

Harness

Used in either a waist or seat style, the harness takes the load off the sailors arms by allowing them to hook into the lines on the boom.

Harness Line

The loop fixed on either side of the boom into which the windsurfer hooks his harness.

Head

The top of the sail.

Head Up

To alter course to point further upwind.

Heat exhaustion/ Heat stroke

Conditions where your body is unable to cope with being overheated; occurs if you are dehydrated and physically active in a hot environment.

Helicopter tack

Freestyle manoeuvre. Basically a tack in which where your body and the rig rotate through 270 degrees, rather than the minimum 180, for added flourish!

Hypothermia

A situation where you have lost sufficient body heat for your core temperature to start to drop. A very dangerous condition.

IMCS

Indexed Mast Check System. The best recognised method of calibrating the stiffness characteristics of windsurfing masts.

Indoor Windsurfing

Indoor windsurfing competition started in the Bercy Stadium, Paris in 1989; recently revived at the London boat show in 2004. Basically, it is sailing a big pool with a row of huge fans providing the wind..

IYRU

The International Yacht Racing Union (responsible for the Olympic class of windsurfing).

Knot

A measurement of speed. A nautical mile per hour. I knot = 1.15mph.

Laydown Gybe

A type of racing gybe, where the rig is laid down flat into the turn for a few seconds, decreasing wind resistance and allowing the sailor to really lean into the turn. Handy if sailing very overpowered!

Leech

The back, or trailing edge of the sail, between the head and the clew.

Leeward

Downwind direction from the board.

Loft

A sail loft is anywhere used for building sails (including basements!).

Loop

(Forward , backward or double!) Extreme aerial manoeuvre.

Long Board

Generally taken to mean boards of over 320cm.

Luff

The leading edge of the sail from the head to the tack. The luff tube contains the mast. Luffing refers to when the sail is starting to flutter because the wind is hitting it from both sides like a flag.

Mast Extension

Made of aluminium or carbon tubing, most extensions offer a range of different settings enabling a mast to be lengthened to accept larger sails.

Mastfoot

The piece that slots into the bottom of the mast and to which the sail is connected. The mast foot itself then slots onto the UJ and deckplate.

Mast Track

The slot in the deck to which the deck plate is fastened; the deck-plate can be moved fore or aft to suit the sailors preference.

Minibattens

Short battens or multilayered strips of fabric used to stiffen the leech of a sail in the softer areas to minimise flutter.

Monofilm

Clear material widely used in sails.

Neoprene

Rubber-based material used for the manufacture of wetsuits, boots and gloves.

No Nose

Generic term describing boards with lower volume noses.

Offshore Wind

A wind blowing from the land to the sea.

Off the Lip

An advanced wave sailing manoeuvre off the breaking lip of a wave.

Olympic Board

There is one design class for the Olympics, which is being decided about now...

Olympic Triangle

The triangle course has three legs, with corners in an equilateral triangle. The first leg is straight upwind. For most windsurfing the more modern 'M' shape or rectangular 'box' course is preferred.

One Design

A few boards race as identical one-designs to remove any equipment advantage, making it totally a test of the sailor's skill. The bic Techno class races are an example. The Olympics uses the same criteria.

Onshore Wind

A wind that's blowing onto the shore.

Outhaul

Line to pull the clew of the sail tight to the back of the boom.

Overpowered

Sailing where the wind is too strong to be completely comfortable for the sail size you are using, and it would be possible to use a smaller sail if desired. However, many folk prefer to sail this way anyway, and racers will almost always sail extremely overpowered, so that if the wind lulls they still have power to spare.

Phazer

Slang for a grooved undersurface, seen on some radical freestyle boards.

Plane/Planing

Skimming across the top of the water, rather than sailing through it ('displacing') as a ship does.

Polyethylene/ Polypropolene

Tough plastic skin materials. Most manufacturers using blow-moulded construction will utilise a mix of these two materials.

Port

Left. The port tack means left shoulder forward.

Power Box

A fin box system.

Pulleyhook

A small hook for the tack cringle (downhaul fixing point) with 3/4 pulley wheels. Allows you to keep the downhaul permanently threaded through the pulleyhook, giving a 6:1 or 8:1 advantage.

Quiver

Collective term used to describe a selection of boards, sails or fins. A full 'quiver' of sails will consist of a number of different sizes to cater for a range of conditions.

Rail

The edges of the board.

Railing

Sailing fast with the daggerboard down; the extra lift created will tend to heel the board over onto its edge. The technique is regularly used by long board racers to sail much faster upwind; as there is less of the board in contact with the water, drag is heavily reduced.

Reaching

Sailing at around 90 degrees to the wind (crosswind).

Reduced Diameter Mast (RDM)

'Skinnies'. A type of mast that is much narrower.

Regatta

A competition meeting with a series of races and events.

Rig

The mast, mastfoot, sail and boom combined.

Rip

A fast flowing current within a body of water. Rips can be very dangerous, especially when swimming, or when they flow through a narrow gap in a reef, for example.

Roach

The area of the leech outside a straight line drawn from head to clew.

Rocker

The curve of the underside of the board as it lifts towards the nose (sometimes known as 'scoop').

Rotational

A fully battened sail with no cams, a rotational relies on the wind force (and a quick shake from the sailor) to flip the battens around the mast and deform into the airfoil section on the other side. Sometimes known as RAF (rotating airfoil) sails.

Running

Sailing with the wind directly behind you. Not a very efficient point of sailing.

Sandwich Construction

A composite construction method, utilising a thin 'sandwich' layer of high density foam between the low-density foam core and the outer skin.

Scoop

Another name for nose rocker.

Set (waves)

Waves will normally occur in 'sets' of between three and eight.

Shorebreak

Used to describe waves that break close in or directly onto the shore.

Shorty (wetsuit)

One with thinner neoprene and short arms and legs for warmer water.

Shoulder

The unbroken part of a breaking wave.

Sideshore

The same as cross-shore.

Simulator

A board mounted on a turntable, used by windsurfing schools to teach basic techniques.

Sinker

A board with low volume (i.e. will sink if you slow down or stop).

Skeg

Another word for a fin (commonly used by surfers).

Slalom

High speed course racing in planing conditions, usually without any upwind legs.

Slot

The 'slot' is the gap between the foot of the sail and the deck of the board.

Slot Flusher

A slot flusher or gasket is two strips of plastic at the bottom of the daggerboard case, to seal the gap and prevent water gushing up through the daggerboard slot.

Spin Out

If the pressure and the angle of attack of the fin is too great, the fin will 'stall' and lose its grip causing the tail to 'spin out'. It generally afflicts short boards travelling at speed through chop.

Spock

Advanced freestyle move; a derivative of the 'Vulcan', hence its name.

Spreader Bar

An aluminium or stainless steel bar attached to the harness which spreads the load taken by the hook.

Starboard

Right. The starboard tack is when your right shoulder is leading. (Also the name of a leading manufacturer).

Steamer

A warm (usually 5mm body) full wetsuit.

Stringers

Longitudinal reinforcement strips to add strength and stiffness to a board.

Table Top

An aerial manoeuvre in which the board ends up above the sailor.

Tack

The corner of the sail at the bottom of the mast.

Tacking

Changing course by pushing the nose of the board through the wind.

Tide

Rise and fall of the water level of the sea due to the gravitational pull of the sun and moon.

Thrusters

Small fins either side of the main fin common on surfboards and sometimes used on wave boards.

Trim Box

Bolt through fin box system that allows a small degree of fin position adjustment.

Towing Eye

A useful thing to have in the nose of the board.

Tuttle Box

A bolt through fin box system using two bolts.

Twinzer

Term for twin fin boards; as fins get ever longer, we are likely to see more twinzer designs.

Twist

The trailing edge of a modern sail (and many modern fins) is designed to 'twist' and release power in the gusts.

Universal Joint (UJ)

Usually a tendon of very tough rubber or a similar material allowing free movement of the mast foot.

Uphaul

A thick knotted rope or elasticated webbing used to pull the rig out of the water.

Volume

The volume of the board determines its buoyancy and weight carrying ability.

Vulcan

A mid air gybe, with the feet staying in the straps. A freestyle move.

Waterstart

A technique used to get back on board easily and quickly after a fall; vital for wave conditions or low volume boards, when up-hauling is not practical.

Wetted Area

The area of the board's bottom which is in contact with the water.

Windward

The side of the board the wind is blowing onto.

Wipe Out

Falling off (should always be done with style).

World Cup

The international racing circuit run by the Professional Windsurfers Association (PWA).

Photo: f8 photography

Appendix 1: Wind Strength Conversion Table

Force	mph	Knots	kph	m/sec	Description	Sea State	Land Indicators
0	<1	<1	<1	0 to 0.2	Calm	Smooth. *Not suitable*	Calm. Smoke rises vertically
1	1 to 3	1 to 3	1 to 5	0.3 to 1.5	Light Air	Ripples, no appearance of scales. No foam crests *Poor for all but initial lessons*	Smoke drift shows direction Vanes do not move
2	4 to 7	4 to 6	6 to 11	1.6 to 3.3	Light Breeze	Small wavelets, smooth crests. *Good training conditions*	Wind felt on face, leaves rustle Vanes move
3	8 to 12	7 to 10	12 to 19	3.4 to 5.4	Gentle Wind	Large wavelets, crests begin to break. *Good training conditions boards with big rigs may plane*	Leaves and small twigs move light flags extend
4	13 to 18	11 to 16	20 to 29	5.5 to 7.9	Moderate Wind	Waves up to 4ft may form, whitecaps evident. *Good planing conditions, tricky for beginners*	Leaves and rubbish blows around, flags flap, small branches move
5	19 to 24	17 to 21	30 to 38	8.0 to 10.7	Fresh Wind	Waves up to 8ft m, many whitecaps, some spray. *Blasting weather!*	Small trees start to sway, flags ripple
6	25 to 31	22 to 27	39 to 50	10.8 to 13.8	Strong Wind	Waves up to 13ft , foaming whitecaps, spray. *Competent sailors only*	Large branches sway, whistling in wires may be heard.
7	32 to 38	28 to 33	51 to 61	13.9 to 17.1	Near Gale	Waves up to 20ft, white foam blown in streaks. *Experts only*	Whole trees in motion, resistance when walking
8	39 to 46	34 to 40	62 to 74	17.2 to 20.7	Gale	Waves up to 20ft. Edges of crests break. Dense foam streaks. *Nuclear! Risky!*	Trees in motion, strong resistance to walking.
9	47 to 54	41 to 27	75 to 86	20.8 to 24.4	Strong Gale	Rolling seas, waves, foam and spray are evident. *Not suitable.*	Slight structural damage occurs.

Index